Mrs LC's Table

Anoothi Vishal is a columnist and writer, specializing in food history, trends and the business of restaurants. She also curates experiences to showcase traditional cuisines of India, including the Kayasth food of her family.

Mrs LC's Table

STORIES ABOUT KAYASTH FOOD AND CULTURE

ANOOTHI VISHAL

hachette INDIA

First published in 2016 by Hachette India
(Registered name: Hachette Book Publishing India Pvt. Ltd)
An Hachette UK company
www.hachetteindia.com

SRD

ISBN 978-93-5009-565-2

Hachette Book Publishing India Pvt. Ltd
4th/5th Floors, Corporate Centre,
Sector 44, Gurgaon 122003, India

Typeset in Apollo MT Std 11.5/16.3
by InoSoft Systems Noida

MIX
Paper from
responsible sources
FSC™ C104740

To Aaliya

'Tell me what you eat, and I will tell you what you are.'

- Jean Anthelme Brillat-Savarin,

The Physiology of Taste (1825)

Contents

The imperious Mrs LC

Introduction

A Reluctant Gourmet – and a Reluctant Kayasth

My grandmother, Swaroop Rani Mathur, was only a reluctant gourmet for she certainly didn't consider herself to be one. Instead, she admitted to being a fussy eater, a special-occasions-only cook and conveniently left all the experimenting with new, unknown foods and other adventures to her husband, Lakshmi Chandra Mathur – or LC, as his Railways colleagues addressed him – widely regarded as a person of refined sensibilities and palate.

I remember a meal I organized for the family – the entire extended clan – at what I regarded at the time as the best Indian restaurant in Delhi. This was soon after I had started writing on food and restaurants for the *Indian Express*. My father had indulgently asked me to choose a place where he could take everyone out for dinner. A newly minted 'expert', I was conscious of my responsibility, keen to find approval for the food I chose and consequently for myself. A new restaurant with a rather unusual menu had just opened at one of the hotels. I thought the dishes were cooked brilliantly. There were few clichés of Indian restaurant cooking. Instead, regional food, both from bazaars and homes, found fair representation. I was confident everyone would be wowed.

They were. Except for my beloved grandmother – known to others as Mrs LC and to us as Barima – who sat through the entire meal with just a bowl of strawberry ice cream. That was all she would eat.

The menu was short and compact, there weren't too many options to choose from, and nothing on it met my picky grandmother's fancy. Neither the kurkuri bhindi, crisply fried ladies' finger, nor the lentils, of which the kali urad, black lentils, was in any case banned from Barima's table (it was regarded as inauspicious, to be cooked and consumed only during times of mourning), and certainly not the baghare baigan, the Hyderabadi-style preparation of eggplant.

Barima had strong likes and dislikes, at least when it came to food (with people she was more accommodating). Baigan, unfortunately, fell into the category of ingredients that she could hardly lay her eyes on, much less stomach. Even though it was my grandfather's favourite vegetable and was cooked quite frequently – with kalonji (onion seeds), or a stuffing of dry masala (saunf and amchoor, that is, fennel seeds and dry mango powder) – Barima remained immune to its charms. The squishiness of the cooked vegetable put her off even before the taste. So strong was her distaste, in fact, that she refused to eat anything that had been 'touched' by the vegetable. We certainly dared not use the spoon with which baigan had been ladled on to our plates to serve Barima her meal! As a strict vegetarian and in keeping with the religious mores observed by many 'upper-caste' Hindus of her time, Barima would also, of course, not eat meat. Like eggplant, meat preparations too had to be kept away from her plate, on the other side of the dining table. In her home, the family always abided by the custom of cooking meat in a separate set of utensils, even though it was cooked routinely and sat quite happily on the common dining table, side by side with the vegetarian fare.

However, despite the dietary restrictions, despite her fussiness, and despite the fact that she only cooked selectively and did not consider herself to be exceptionally interested in food, Mrs LC *was* a gourmet. For one, her table was always deliciously laden. Yakhni pulao, shami kebab, sookhi urad dal, kofte, bharwan bhindi, papad aloo, takey paise, makhane ki kheer, gajar ka halwa, pooris and parathas, bedmi–aloo, seasonal pickles – many of these dishes were served almost daily for lunch or dinner. Both elaborately cooked seasonal vegetables of her choice and slow-cooked meat dishes appeared with fair regularity on the table, many of them treated as centrepieces of the family meals.

Though neither of my grandparents ate meat, much of the clan did, with great delight. LC, whom I called Papa, had been a meat eater in his younger days, and an enthusiastic one too, but had turned vegetarian by the time I came along. Barima, on the other hand, followed Vaishnavite rituals, read the 'Sundar Kanda', the shortest and most beautifully composed chapter of the *Ramcharitmanas* by Tulsidas, every day, fasted frequently and stuck to her vegetarian moorings. Yet, for the rest of the family, there was no taboo regarding meat eating. Cooking meat was, in fact, almost elevated to an art form.

Whenever dining table conversations turned to the merits or demerits of the kofte or kaliya, both traditionally made from lamb meat and staples of the clan, my grandmother would enthusiastically join in, pronouncing her verdict. She, who had never tasted these dishes in her life, felt competent to weigh in on such matters. This did not seem exceptional or even worthy of comment to any of us because, as with most Kayasth women of her time, not eating meat did not stop my grandmother from *cooking* it. She could cook perfectly without tasting and this almost instinctive knowledge – or rather, talent – made her an expert alright. Mrs LC's shami kebabs were legendary. They were not of the chunky-patty kind, but delicate ones, stuffed with mint and onions, and soft enough to be galawat ke kebab, even though no tenderizer by way of raw papaya or some such such was ever added to soften the goat mince. It was the recipe – the proportion of chana dal used to bind the mince – that made all the difference. The proportions and the recipe were verbally passed down to daughters and daughters-in-law, and the family still follows them strictly. Her recipe for yakhni pulao was equally sought-after. Cooked in the yakhni, or stock, itself, the pulao was superbly fragrant, the subtle taste of the stock infusing each grain of Basmati rice. Yakhni pulao was a keenly anticipated Sunday lunch ritual, much more than the kachche keeme ke kofte, the other meat dish popular among Kayasth families. Like Mrs LC, most Kayasth matriarchs were vegetarians. Yet, the keema kofte would be cooked with the flair, perfection and ease resulting from years of practice.

It wasn't only the women in the family who picked up the nuances of cooking these dishes. My father, Rajeev, the LCs' eldest son, turned out to be an outstanding hobby cook – a discovery that was made once he relaxed his workaholic routine and started frequenting the kitchen more often, after his mother's death. In fact, it will be fair to say that both Mrs LC and my father can be considered fair representatives of the Kayasth flair for food and cooking. While they were and are individualistic in their culinary expressions, their interest and dexterity in the art demonstrates the continuance of a long tradition. Both Kayasth men and women have always had formidable reputations as instinctive cooks. Most have a knack for balancing flavours, spicing and textures, and inventing new and elaborate dishes. They are also known to be gourmets.

Anyone who has been a recipient of Kayasth *khatirdari*, or hospitality, will attest not only to the generosity and warmth that gives it its special quality but also to the community's great preoccupation with food that goes above and beyond the idea of eating merely for sustenance. In traditional Kayasth homes an inordinate amount of time would be spent discussing the day's menu. *'Aaj dinner mein kya ban raha hai?'* ('What's cooking for today's dinner?') was the standard query at a breakfast table overflowing with jalebi, halwa, chhoti pooris, chunki hui matar, shami kebabs or parathas with bhune aloo. Food was quite definitely the focus of a way of life that has been on the wane for a while now, a more leisured way of being, in which living was not merely a process of survival and consumption. In which accumulating material possessions and wealth came second to the many cultural preoccupations; large, extended families shared lives and bonded over rituals of cooking and eating; and, apart from food, the immersion in artistic pursuits loomed large.

If kebabs and pulao were the focal points of many social interactions in Kayasth homes like that of my grandparents, so were music and *shayari*, or poetry. It was pretty much a given that both men and women were trained in Hindustani classical music. Teachers, who were respectfully called 'guruji' or 'masterji', would come home to train girls in vocal music or in playing the sitar, and the men often knew how to play the tabla if not any other instrument. Festivals, weddings, community gatherings and other occasions were opportunities to display one's talent. Many like my grandfather and his brothers wrote verse in Urdu, and later Hindi, with great felicity. Some participated in *mushairas*, or poetry gatherings, others wrote plays or took to amateur theatre. All art, including food and music, was entertainment.

On the flipside, like many closed societies, this world could be a suffocating one too, with its emphasis on manners and politeness, on nuanced behaviour that was prized over displays of emotion or candidness. Everything was measured, much remained unspoken. Individualism or questioning was barely tolerated and displays of temper, rebellion or disobedience of inherited patterns were rare. The Kayasth world may have been culturally unique but it was also a world that expected and propagated cultural conformity. Like many courtly and semi-courtly cultures, it was a patriarchal world too, despite the fact that Kayasth women were mostly educated and were among the first women in India to embrace 'Western' education in schools and colleges.

This preoccupation with 'culture' and the sense of superiority most Kayasth families exhibited as the self-styled custodians of a refined way of life would often make me – someone who had seen both the LCs' world and its gradual collapse with the emergence of a newer, cosmopolitan, globalized order – impatient. Even fifteen years ago, when Barima was still alive, if someone had suggested that I would be writing a book on all things Kayasth, I would have scoffed at the idea. I was the quintessential misfit who had been born into a particular culture-scape but was incessantly seeking to escape it. I disliked tradition, sought to escape the rigours of learning Hindustani classical music imposed upon me by the family's zeal for it and certainly did not want to get married within the community as per Barima's dearest, long-standing wish. While I ate our *khana*, food, enthusiastically enough, I had no desire to slave over the preparation of intricate Kayasth meat and vegetarian recipes when I could be profitably spending my time doing other things. Increasingly, as that world recedes faster than ever before, I find myself inclined to go back to it, at least in memory, and as I begin to examine the origins of that world, the multiplicity of layers that constitute it, the richness of my heritage becomes obvious.

I don't know if others in the community realize that Kayasths, even families like mine that always sought to reiterate the homogeneity of their culture, may actually be the first examples of the subcontinent's syncretic Ganga–Jamuni heritage: a way of life spawned by the coming together of different cultural strands. No firm records of their origins, history and culture exist – as is common in India where, throughout our history, the oral tradition has been stronger than the written one. Nevertheless, it seems strange to me that no one from this community of scribes that thrived on the might of their pen and ink thought of recording their lineage and lifestyle. Various accounts ascribe the origin of the Kayasth community to Mathura,

Agra and other towns of UP near and around Delhi. There are several theories about the genesis of the Kayasths, and I will recount some of them in a subsequent chapter of this book. But one thing is certain. As a community, the Kayasths were not a part of the original varna system of Vedic society. They seem to have emerged on their own as a culturally distinct community in medieval India, around the time of the early Mughals. Courtiers to the Mughal emperors, the Kayasths started out as record keepers, literate in Persian, the language of the rulers. Proximity with Mughal culture meant that the customs, language, attire, speech, lifestyle and, of course, cuisine of the courtly way of life seeped into the local Hindu cultures of Delhi, Braj and Avadh (in UP), and other parts of the Indo-Gangetic plain.

With the educated elite in demand in the form of accountants, clerks, secretaries and ministers, not just in princely courts but also at the district level, the Kayasth world spread to many other regions of the subcontinent. As families fanned out to other areas, establishing their seats, wielding considerable influence locally, they assimilated regional influences into their way of living. Today, when we look at the Bengali Kayasths or the Maharashtrian Kayasths or indeed families from Hyderabad and Bihar, it is obvious that each of them has a fairly distinct culture, imbued with very strong local colour and flavour.

Meat eating and cooking in the community – particularly among men, who were closer to the courtly culture by virtue of their work, while the women mostly stuck to their religious roots – is only one part of the larger Ganga–Jamuni fabric. In fact, it is not just the rich (and famous) non-vegetarian culinary repertoire of Kayasth cuisine – kaliya, kofta, bhuna meat, badam pasanda, shami kebab, yakhni pulao – that reflects the admixture with Mughal culture. In my view, it is the community's distinctive vegetarian cooking that underlines the cultural intermingling far better. Vegetables are often treated like meat, *bhuna* (slow-roasting in fat) and *dum* (steam-cooking) being two common cooking techniques applied equally to vegetarian and non-vegetarian cooking. Interestingly, there is also a well-developed strand of 'faux meat' dishes to appease vegetarians, particularly the ladies of the house. These range from vegetarian kofte, made from every seasonal vegetable conceivable, to *naqli* (fake) omelettes and even kaleji (liver) ki subzi, made from lentils seeking to approximate the flavour and texture of curried liver. Such culinary creations are a direct outcome of a cultural confluence.

Fresh elements were added with the coming of colonial rule, with the Kayasths adapting once again to a new ruling class and incorporating much of the new manners and lifestyle into their fabric. From their origins as scribes, the Kayasths went on to become part of the administrative echelons, such as the judiciary and revenue services. In some parts of the country, primarily eastern UP, Bihar and Bengal, they became landlords, by virtue of land and largesse bestowed upon them by the rulers in return for being staunch loyalists. The British – to whom the Kayasths turned, with all the power of their pens, after the decline of the original masters, the Mughals – were particularly generous in this regard.

With the coming of the British, as members of the community embraced the English language, climbed the ranks in the civil services, became teachers in universities, and joined the Railways and the Post and Telegraph services, their lifestyle changed once more. From Mughal-inspired living, other mores now seeped into the ever-assimilating cultural fabric of the Kayasths. Drinking 'bed tea' out of fine porcelain (Hindu homes had until then used only 'pure' metal utensils made of silver or an alloy called 'phool'), eating at a dining table (which replaced the low *chowkis* or stools in the kitchen) and drinking whisky every evening became a customary ritual in Kayasth homes, at least among the 'upper' classes. So entrenched did this last custom become that today it is difficult to imagine any Kayasth khana without *peena*, drink – shami kebab without an accompanying peg of Scotch, for instance.

It would be a mistake to examine Kayasth – or any – food in isolation. For most communities, cooking is a way of expressing their identity. Kayasth cuisine is doubly interesting because the uniqueness of the community arises from it being a blend of several different identities, and Kayasth food reveals this in many interesting ways. If I had to pick one word to describe the nature of Kayasth culture, it would be 'assimilation' – right from the early Mughal period through to the British rule. Kayasth food and culture can, in fact, be seen as the original attempt at 'fusion' – even though it is not a term I like to use in the context of food. I find the simplest of eating traditions within the community – like the pairing of Mughal-influenced kofte or kebabs with fried pooris, regarded as ritualistic food in Hindu communities – reflecting this sense of 'fusion' or amalgamation of identities.

Inventiveness and adaptability, the two most important traits of the community, its culture and cuisine, best explain how the community survived and thrived. From being 'upper-class', *shaukeen* Mughal-like aristocrats, who moulded their colourful cultural preoccupations on the lines of their Mughal or Nawabi employers (if Muhammed Shah 'Rangeela' and 'Zafar' could be consumed by poetry and music, so could many Kayasths of good taste and standing) to being the 'brown sahibs', Kayasths seem to have shifted allegiance seamlessly, adopting newer ways of living while retaining their older practices. Traditional Hindu beliefs and rituals were happily woven into the fabric of their lives along with courtly Mughal pastimes and the more 'modern' manners of nineteenth-century Victorianism. If the dining table – along with the bevy of 'butlers', servers and cooks employed at the LCs' bureaucratic homes, fancy dinner sets, cutlery and manners – was a legacy of the Raj, the food on that table reflected other zones of being. Bedmi–aloo, chhoti poori, shami kebab, yakhni pulao, keema kofta and a whole host of *naqli* dishes paid tribute to the creativity and dexterity of the 'chefs' in the family, in whose veins ran an intriguing legacy.

In this book I seek to illustrate the essence of Kayasth culture by placing the food on Barima's table firmly in a larger context. More comprehensive sociological research may throw up links between different Kayasth communities and sub-castes spread across different parts of India. I have tried to draw out some of these fascinating links through the foods of a handful of Kayasth families other than mine. But this account is largely confined to the Kayasth culture of Delhi and UP, home to my ancestor Munshi Shivlal, an eighteenth-century record-keeper from Moradabad, to whom my paternal Mathur family traces its lineage. I have told the story of the community and its food through the prism of my memories of Mrs LC, the reluctant gourmet and enthusiastic musician, my beloved grandmother, whose world constantly collided with mine. Until now.

PART I

THE KAYASTH WORLD

Who are the Kayasths?

That is a tricky question. It is also perhaps one that is not very important. What really matters is that the Kayasth way of life – and their cuisine, as an intrinsic part of it – is one of the truest manifestations of India's splendid Ganga–Jamuni culture: the blending of Indo-Islamic influences, resulting in a rich, layered tapestry, an expression of the idea of a syncretic, 'secular' India. But while the coming together of two distinct cultural strands is obvious in the speech, style of dressing, customs and indeed cuisine of older Kayasth families, this social integration was selective at best and the religious barrier was rarely breached. We may tend to idealize this Ganga–Jamuni culture and cuisine, but it is important to realize that, much like every social reality in India, the Kayasth reality is quite complex. In the Kayasth worldview, there has always been a deep sense of discomfort with the 'other', of cultural superiority rather than a recognition of Kayasth way of life as a confluence of cultural strands.

Being 'Kayasth' certainly did not define me in the way it defined my grandparents and my parents. I took no pride in the conceits of the community passed down through generations. The breakdown of the joint family and changing times meant that we lived in a much more open world compared to that of our parents; there were newer, more exciting influences, friends and peers who did not belong to the same caste, whose food and language and thoughts were different. To me, the *khana–pakana–gana* (eating–cooking–singing) lifestyle of the LCs, with its emphasis on *tameez*, of conducting oneself properly all the time, seemed cloistered, limited. But even as I felt split between the outer world – of my friends, of exams interrupted by the Mandal Commission and the Babri Masjid demolition and of the innumerable new thrills that youth brings – and the inner world of my family, I would always come back to Barima, her intense affection for me, her stories. And, unknowingly, I breathed in the continuum of culture and the Kayasth way of life that had existed for centuries.

1

Raags, Recipes and Rebellion

Memories

Vasudevan Uncle was convinced I was pulling a fast one on him. 'Why,' he spluttered, all fumes and filter coffee, 'do you want the entire day off? Everyone only celebrates Dussehra in the evening.'

Mr Vasudevan, "uncle" to me, was my maths tutor. His fierce reputation as a taskmaster in Lucknow made it difficult to counter his logic. Every year, he handpicked a select batch of ICSE students, explaining to them elusive concepts in physics, chemistry and maths, sending them hurtling on to a path of sweat and glory. To be accepted into Mr Vasudevan's tutorial guaranteed a good, even great result in the board exams. To make it to his super-exclusive batch meant you would be among the all-India toppers. His reputation was *that* solid. And it was natural he would want to protect it.

As one of the four students he had singled out for his select batch, I owed him all my time. The Sunday movie on Doordarshan, the 9 p.m. soap operas, *Chitrahaar*, every form of recreation including family outings, reading of 'frivolous' books, all forms of sports – all of it had to be sacrificed at the altar of PCM, the sacred combination of Physics–Chemistry–Maths he wanted me to ace. Naturally inclined towards literature as I was, these subjects were not my strength but Vasudevan Uncle made sure I was good enough to beat the best. Almost.

Openly telling him I would not be coming for the class on Dussehra was thus tantamount to treachery – the sounding of a revolt in his tightly administered kingdom. I was in danger of being expelled from my tutorial group, with my board exams less than five months away. But how could I explain to Vasudevan Uncle my compulsions? The call of the kaliya? The allure of aloo kachoris?

No, Dussehra was not about exploding Ravana's effigy at dusk. I don't think that bit fascinated me, even as a child. For me and everyone in my family, it was the daytime rituals that were all-consuming. The careful smearing of the *aipan*, the auspicious paste of flour and turmeric, on pens and books; the writing of a verse from the Ramayana on a fraying old sheet of paper (my grandfather made it a point to write it in Urdu, the continuation of a centuries-old syncretic tradition); the frying of aloo kachoris made for Hanuman, able aide of Ram; eating a grand lunch, carefully scooping up dark brown kaliya that had been slow-cooked for hours in the pot with sizzling hot pooris; and then snoozing, sated, till the effigies and fireworks exploded at dusk.

How, could I, at fifteen, have even begun to explain the hold of these strange customs on me? The sense of piousness, the flavour of the meat, the satiation, the pull of centuries-old rituals that resided in my blood and that would call out to me – however much I tried running away from it? And I did try...

❋

'Sing,' whispered Barima, looking frail and broken on the hospital bed, the antithesis of the strong grandmother I knew and loved. 'Sing that song...'

I closed my eyes and began to sing in the hospital room.

Jhunak Shyam ki paijaniya
Jhunak Shyam ki paijaniya
Shyam baran par, peet jhanguria...

(The tinkling of Shyam's anklets
The tinkling of Shyam's anklets
Enchants, as
The yellow attire on his dark body...)

The strong smell of disinfectants had made me pass out just as I had reached the floor in the hospital, straight from work, hurried, nervous about the condition in which I would find my beloved grandmother. A rather amused young resident doctor had helped me back on my feet before getting back to his task of treating patients. Barima had suffered a massive stroke the night before while talking to my aunt, discussing the prospect of my marriage with some pedigreed Kayasth – a fate I had steadfastly refused to succumb to ever since I had turned twenty, secretly dating boyfriends 1 and 2. And now, inside me, love, concern and guilt were all jumbled up – feelings that wouldn't go away however much I retched. The smell of disinfectant still hung about the room, but as I sang my grandmother our favourite bhajan – it grew faint.

Lost in the gentle, repetitive melody, in a way I seldom am when facing an audience, even the kindest, I felt grief, stress and other unrecognized feelings ooze out of me. I sobbed out the last stanza. Barima looked at peace, drifting off to sleep. It was the last song she would ever teach me, the stroke robbing her of coherent thought and words for years afterwards. But I didn't know that just yet. And, having wept at her frailty and mine, I felt at peace.

Barima was the most determined person I knew, and the most imperious. I have vivid images of my grandmother supervising in the kitchen – an impressive, commanding presence who expected things to be done a certain way and got them done through the sheer force of her personality, without anyone creating fuss or raising dissent. Her father, Abbaji, had worked as the revenue minister in Gwalior, under Jivaji Rao Scindia, and later as the prime minister of various other princely states. As a result, Barima had

had a semi-royal upbringing in a feudal, pre-independence India. Yet, rather than be content with this life, she was a rebel of sorts.

In the tonga that used to ferry her sister and her to school every morning – following an hour of musical *riyaaz* (practice) that their mother insisted on – Barima was never the timid passenger. At some point between home and school, she would insist on taking over the reins, ordering the hapless tonga-walla to move aside. He dare not complain, and the family never got to know of such incidents. Later, as an undergraduate student in a girls' hostel, she insisted on her own car (this time, with a chauffeur) and a personal cook, and was prone to much socializing, a habit that did not leave her till the very end.

She married my grandfather, Lakshmi Chandra Mathur, from the same 'high' Kayasth sub-caste but not exactly in keeping with the wishes of Abbaji, who wanted a more moneyed groom for his darling daughter. LC was good-looking and had a stable enough job with the Indian Railways, and so, despite his relatively modest background, she married him, devoting her considerable skills to furthering his bureaucratic career – striking friendships, networking (though that was not a term she used or knew), singing ghazals at club functions, *banna-banni*s (playful songs in praise of the bride and groom) and *mehndi*s (special songs sung during the henna ceremony) at weddings, or lyrics penned by my grandfather set to film music of the 1950s and 60s, administering the various Mathur *sabha*s (community gatherings) in the assorted UP towns the couple lived in, and generally enjoying the limelight.

For her wedding, Barima's heart was set on a beautiful red and gold dinner set that she wanted as part of her trousseau. But those being the royal colours, the dinner set was not for sale to commoners. Not to be denied, Barima, all of nineteen, set about convincing the shopkeeper to let her buy the crockery. And he did. Barima could be supremely persuasive. The only reason I gave in to learning music – Hindustani classical – from 'Masterji', who came home to teach me, was because of Barima. Music was her passion. She had a Visharad degree from the prestigious Allahabad-based institute of Hindustani classical music, Prayag Sangeet Samiti. For her, music was much more than an expression of talent. It was the continuance of tradition, the reaffirmation and transmission of a legacy and a unique way of life to a younger generation, at a time when it was increasingly losing its relevance.

I am not sure how much of this Barima actually realized. She was the product of a milieu where music was mandatory in Mathur households. Every girl was expected to be accomplished in the art – in singing, or at least playing an instrument – and, frequently, many boys were deeply entrenched in it too. People wrote verses in Urdu, there was *shayari* and theatre, open houses hosted musicians and artistes. It was this sense of being 'cultured' that separated the elite, courtly Mathur Kayasths from the hoi polloi, she believed. My aunts and my mother were partly raised with the same sense of 'Mathur-ness' as something distinct and more desirable than what the neighbours had. But by the time I came along, India was changing. It was a more equal society, Bollywood and cricket were levellers, film and rock music were the preferred choices, and I could hardly break into a raag – or even a bhajan or geet, taught to me as subsidiary 'light music' after the khayals had been practised in classes with Masterji, when asked to sing in my social group.

As a seven-year-old I was far from inclined to 'waste' my time learning sargam, alaap and Raag Yaman after school while all my friends were busy playing in the park outside. Plus, Masterji was hardly a likeable character. He was stern and grouchy, an old-fashioned guru, not given to making any allowances for children. 'So, you ate ice cream again?' he would accuse me, and be offended by the fact that I hadn't practised enough. He was the bane of my existence; I dreamt of chasing him away, throwing potatoes and onions at him, but I dared not miss a class because of the influence Barima wielded on me.

It wasn't that I feared Barima. It was just that I didn't want to disappoint her. She was never strict. On the contrary, she was the most indulgent human being I have ever known. Barima had taken charge of my care when I was a toddler, bringing me to Banaras, where my grandfather was then posted as a fairly high-ranking official in the Northern Railways. My parents had their hands full after the birth of my twin brother and sister, two years after I was born. The love she lavished upon me is legendary in the family annals. True to her own feudal upbringing, she brought me up in a manner that can only be likened to that of a 'railway princess'. While waiting for my school bus in the morning, I sat on a small chair set out at the bus stand for my comfort, a member of the staff holding an umbrella over me to shelter me from the sun. Before I bathed, the entire bathroom would be washed. When I slept, Barima would keep my slippers under her pillow, lest I find them too cold to wear in the morning!

She also told me stories. By the time I was four, I knew all the intricate subplots of the Ramayana and Mahabharata, well enough to engage older friends of my grandparents with their narration. I also knew considerable trivia, such as in which year bridge over the Ganga had collapsed, which waiting room at which railway station served the best egg curry, or, for that matter, the exact recipe for gajar ka halwa, one of the many dishes that were my grandmother's speciality.

'In one kilo of carrots, add two litres of milk and cook well. Then add half a kilo of sugar...' The proportions were casually narrated to me like a bedtime story and they stayed with me even though I haven't made gajar ka halwa till date. In any case, I have never come across anyone who makes the dessert exactly like Barima did. Unlike the bazaar-bought halwas, or those made in other homes, Barima's trick was to keep it simple in terms of ingredients and laborious in terms of the actual cooking. No khoya, or condensed milk, was to be added – that would have been sacrilege. Instead, the grated carrot was cooked in full-fat milk and on a low flame for the longest possible time, constantly watched and stirred, especially as the milk reduced, the carrot soaking it all up. It was taken off the fire only after it turned dark red and had a consistency at which the halwa could be set on thalis and cut into thin katlis (we didn't call them barfis). This was a winter special – savoured, prized, a favourite with all my grandmother's children, to whom special boxes were sent each winter.

It was also one of the few things my imperious grandmother actually cooked herself. Unlike fictional and other real grannies, Barima was hardly the kind to slave it over the kitchen fire. Indeed, so hectic was her social life at one point that she would communicate with her children through notes kept by her bedside. (All her children grew up undamaged and adoring her.) She kept an impeccable table, was very particular about what she ate and how, but when it came to cooking there were just a few specials that she deigned to cook herself – leaving the staff and, later, her daughters-in-law to follow her recipes.

Of the dishes she cooked, margul – arvi or colocasia wrapped in a dry, grated onion-based masala and pan-fried on a tawa, on a low flame – was one she loved. There was also pakori ki subzi, her absolute favourite – moong dal fritters, super soft and tender, dunked in a thin, watery gravy flavoured with asafoetida. She would have this with crisp, triangular parathas for dinner and on days when she was breaking a fast, Barima would sit, surrounded by her children and grandchildren, feeding us all small bites from her plate, while an endless supply of karare, crisp, parathas came out of the kitchen.

Barima was an intuitive cook, instinctively knowing the measure of spices, of seasoning; she never went wrong, as far as I can remember, however vast or small the quantity of food being cooked. One strange rituals she followed in the kitchen was to put three pinches of ingredients into a dish – salt, sugar, haldi (turmeric powder), dhaniya (coriander) powder, mirch (red chilli) powder and so on. Three pinches of any seasoning ensured that the measure was always right. Always exact. The pinches could vary in size according to the portions being cooked, but the *teen ka totka*, or three-times ritual, remained the same. Her gift of intuition worked in other situations things as well. Before each important exam her children took as students, they would urge their mother to 'have a dream'. She would dream of the entire question paper and ask her children whether they knew the relevant answers before their exams. From what I have heard, those very questions would appear in the papers the next day!

My father, almost as fine a cook as my grandmother and just as intuitive, follows the same *teen ka totka* and gets it right too, each time. Even though no one in the family has ever really discussed this method of cooking with each other, it seems to have been passed down through generations – whether through the bloodline or observation,

I can't say. For years, I cooked like that too, oblivious of the fact that the *teen ka totka* was a family charm of sorts. It was only when I began to observe my father cooking that the realization hit me. Some of that charm seems to have stopped working for me ever since – or, perhaps, I am just a very temperamental cook!

'I won't marry him, even if he is the last man on this planet!' I told the family – and with that all hell broke loose. A solemn, grim atmosphere descended on the otherwise festive Holi gathering.

Holi has generally been a fun occasion for the family. In the past, my grandparents would have attended a *mushaira* on the occasion, where men pitted their wits and verses against each other. There would have been a Mathur sabha, with music, the singing of *holi* (traditional songs passed down through generations), snacks like gujjas, besan papdi and chaat being shared, lucky dips, unlucky dunking in *haudis* (water tanks found in most old-style bungalows) and boisterous chatting, much of it revolving around matchmaking.

As bigger families broke up and people moved to the metros, Rang Paashi was all that remained of the old festivities. An evening of food and music before the actual festival of colours, Rang Paashi was ushered in by daughters- and sons-in-law putting a little gulal on the elders. Those who were musically inclined, keen on tradition

My grandfather (centre) and his brothers at the ancestral home in Deputy Ganj, Moradabad

and perhaps a little socially competitive, usually sang a couple of *holis*.

Barima insisted that her four children, with families in tow, celebrate each festival together. The joint family had split up long before I was born, and the ancestral home in Deputy Ganj in Moradabad, Raghunath House – meaning the abode of the descendants of Rama, to whom our Avadhi family traced its lineage – had been partitioned and eventually sold off when the last of its patriarchs, my great-grandfather Pradyumn Krishna, died. (He had awaited the birth of a great-grandson so that he could climb the golden staircase to heaven directly from this mortal realm, but was destined to remain eternally disappointed because, instead of the expected heir, a great-granddaughter had come along. My great-grandfather passed away just a month after my birth. It was the passing of an era.)

My grandfather and his brothers had already established homes in different cities. The oldest, KC, who had worked in the Army Headquarters, settled in, the then up-and-coming, Delhi neighbourhood of Greater Kailash. Taiji, or Mrs KC, his talented, loving wife, lavished her maternal care on the Lady Shri Ram girls who took up paying-guest accommodation in a room of their house. PC, the middle brother, a college professor, decided to make Lucknow his base once he retired, spending his days learning and practising music, eating paan and travelling the world. And LC, the youngest, after moving around mofussil towns of

UP, Madhya Pradesh (MP) and Rajasthan as he rose up the ranks in the Railways, settled in a house built by his second son in Ghaziabad, much before the locality became part of the National Capital Region. My grandfather, who had a penchant for unusual names, named the house Abhiram – Ram's home. From here, the LCs would travel every few months to our home in Lucknow, to my youngest uncle's in Cochin, and to other relatives and friends, with an ease born of the pack-and-go Railways life they had always led. For the duration of their stay, that particular home mimicked a joint family set-up, with the clan gathering there for festivals and other family events.

This Holi too was being celebrated en masse. We played gulal and gorged on kaanji bada, or moong dal dumpling, left to ferment and pickle in water that got its tang from fresh mustard, a dish quite unique to Mathur homes, and drank copious amounts of alcohol. Brunch, as always, was baasi parathas and taazi gobi – parathas cooked the night before, with cauliflower freshly sautéed in the morning. But instead of the spirit of lightness that was characteristic of Holi, the mood was tense, heavy and dark.

Jo Shyam aayenge, Brij se palat ke
Holi main khelongi unhi se dat ke
Jo Shyam mose raar karenge sakhi
Gari main doongi, ghungtwa palat ke
Ek hi kumkum, maroongi aisa sakhi
Jo bansiwale ki, jo mohan pyare ki, aankhon me atke

When Shyam comes back from Brij,
I will play Holi with him to my heart's content.
If he teases me while playing with colours, my friend,
I will fling aside my veil and hurl at him words
and vermilion, just once, so passionately
That it clouds the eyes of the flute-player, the charmer,
my beloved.

This was Barima's favourite *holi*. She had taught it to me when she thought I was reasonably adept at the delicate murkis that defined the tune. Every Holi, I dusted the diary she had given me and prepared to sing from it. This year, however, I was not singing. I was sulking, streaks of tears dried dirtily on my face. The family, with all its joint might, was pressurizing me to get married and I was standing firm against it. It hurt, the disapproval of the entire clan.

I had done the unthinkable: refused to meet the pedigreed Mathur boy who my grandmother was keen I marry. No amount of subtle or obvious pressure had worked. I was twenty-one, a trainee sub-editor with a national newspaper, keen to work and party; holy matrimony was far from my mind. To say that the family was upset would be an understatement. (For two years after this, I would not be on talking terms with my father, and remain awkward and angry with the entire extended clan, unwilling to attend get-togethers where I would feel the pressure of unspoken accusations.) Barima, already stricken by crippling arthritis and the stroke that followed, was severely disappointed.

Had my grandmother been a man, she would have been highly successful in whatever profession she chose to pursue. But being a woman in her age and milieu, her considerable ambition turned to other things: to her children and then to me, her first and most loved grandchild. All her three sons owe their careers to Barima. My father, the eldest, always fond of theatre and cooking, was sent to engineering college. My elder chacha, aspiring to be in the Indian Air Force or any of the armed forces, was persuaded to join the merchant navy instead. My younger chacha, luckily, strayed into Roorkee's engineering college without familial pressures.

My aunt, the only daughter of the LCs, was the apple of her parents' eyes. Before she was born, many havans and pujas had been performed by the couple who desperately sought a daughter. Barima wanted nothing short of perfection for her. Educated at an expensive boarding school, possessing the best clothes a bureaucrat's salary could buy, trained in music, art and craft, cooking and baking by whoever was deemed the most proficient in my grandparents' large social circle – my aunt was given all the advantages of attending a finishing school, without actually having been to one. She was raised to marry well, within the community, and she did. Since I had been carefully brought up pretty much on the same principles, Barima's prime ambition for me too was marriage – to a fair, well-placed type, who came from a 'good' family. I chafed against the unjust expectations but patriarchy is so insidious that I didn't even know whether I was justified in chafing against it.

While I wanted to be a journalist for as long as I can remember, my father wanted me to be a bureaucrat. But when he mentioned his civil-service dream for me to my grandmother, she retorted, 'Then when will she get married?' Journalistic aspirations were fine, on the other hand, because everyone quite erroneously believed 'you can always freelance' in the profession – be a part-time writer, a full-time lady-of-leisure. Unknown to the clan, things were changing – and fast. What was the norm in the 1940s, and still passed muster in the 70s, no longer held in the new millennium. Manmohanomics had created a whole new aspirational order. Taxes were lower, the middle class was larger, the first dot-com boom was happening, 'software engineer' had just about taken over 'Indian Administrative Service (IAS) officer' as the preferred tag for Kayasth grooms, people increasingly sold off havelis and bought apartments, foreign travel and foreign education were becoming more common and fewer girls were getting married at twenty-one.

'But we are Mathurs!' said my grandmother with pride, the inference being that we were somehow superior, centuries of 'culture' flowing in our veins. 'All the best Mathur boys get snapped up before they are twenty-five,' she warned, 'and the best girls get married by twenty-three.' It was a ticking time bomb. Get married or stay on the shelf.

Since they considered themselves a cut above the rest of the Kayasths, the Mathurs only married within their small and elite community, and it was considered a disgrace for anyone to have alliances of any other kind. On the other hand, the alliances I sought were strictly of the other kind. Fed on a steady diet of literature, and fuelled by the yearning to be someone else, every cell in my body rebelled against any imposition of Kayasth-ness. Tradition raised my hackles, as did the mere mention of music and marriage. My grandmother may have been behaving exactly like Mrs Bennet, but while the Kayasth social mores may still have been stuck in those times, this was hardly nineteenth-century England. And where was Mr Darcy?

2

A Constantly Changing People

The Origin of the Kayasths

For a long time, I was not conscious of being a Kayasth, or even a Mathur. Growing up in the 1980s–90s, it was not an important part of my identity for me.

Once a year, a day after the festival of Badi Diwali, the family would perform the Chitragupta Puja, much like other Kayasth families do. The highlight of this ceremony was worshipping our pens and inkpots, *kalam* and *dawaat*. We children would enthusiastically bring out our textbooks, school notebooks and pens, and place them at the altar decorated for the puja. It was a small ritual, hardly the highlight of the Diwali festivities, but distinctive enough – though I began to see that only later. Here was a community ritualistically marking out its cultural identity by celebrating literacy. In the same way that agrarian communities have worshipped the plough, till and grinding stones, martial communities their weapons, and traders their scales and ships, the Kayasths bowed down to the tools of our trade, the quill and ink.

Chitragupta Maharaj, said Barima, was the 'founder' of the Kayasth community. But the story began with Yama, the god of death. Yama was always a fierce character in the stories. A harsh judge, he could punish you for the smallest of transgressions. In the kitchen, for instance, my mother would frown upon any of us spilling salt by mistake. In Yama's *narak*, hell, you would be made to pick up all the spilt salt with your eyelashes, she would say. It was a strange Kayasth version of the myth of Sisyphus, I held, but the family elders certainly did not think of it as a joke. Salt was precious. Wasting it, or anything else in the kitchen, was not acceptable. Potatoes and onions had to be thinly peeled, bhindi finely beheaded. These were basic lessons to be learned in Mrs LC's world. God knows what punishments awaited us in the hereafter otherwise.

In any case, to be completely just and keep accounts of all the minor and major transgressions, Yama needed an aide. A keeper of records of virtue and vice, a balance-sheet creator. So Brahma created Chitragupta out of his body, without the help of a woman, through meditation, in secrecy – and this son-sans-a-mother was our family's ancestor. Since Brahma had created Chitragupta solely out of his own body, or *kaya*, Chitragupta's progeny came to be called Kayasths.

Myth and history are not the same thing though both make for fascinating stories, and there are some exceptionally interesting ones floating around on the origin of the Kayasths.

There are no written records tracing the origin and rise of this powerful community of literati that has quasi-governed much of India through centuries. The Kayasths as a community are not mentioned in the later Vedic texts, the epics or the *Manusmriti* (dated second century CE by some historians) which details the varna system in Hindu society. The original varna system divided society into four hierarchical groups, according to the work each carried out: Brahmins (priests), Kshatriyas (warriors), Vaishyas (tradespeople) and Sudras (who supposedly 'served' the first three but were subsequently regarded as 'low caste' in the Brahminical world order). The Kayasths find no mention in this divisive order. It is therefore fair to assume that this community came up as a separate group, or 'caste', much later.

Some accounts claim that Kayasths were the scribes of the Gupta kings of northern India (who ruled between the fourth and sixth centuries CE), and were brought to Bengal by these emperors to help in governance when the Indo-Aryan colonization of the region began. These accounts are also the basis of claims that the Pala kings of Bengal (reigning from the eighth to twelfth centuries CE) were Kayasth. But given the claims that the Palas were the first Buddhist dynasty in the region and the Kayasths' cultural and culinary fabric is definitely non-Buddhist, such assertions appear unreliable.

Then there are oral accounts in the community that

claim ancestry from kshatriya kings. Barima, for instance, would tell us that we were kshatriyas, tracing our lineage to Rama, the king of Ayodhya, a descendant of the sun god. Beyond establishing that ours was a firmly Vaishnavite UP family, these claims always seemed absurd, given that our family, like most of the other Kayasths I knew, was hardly martial. The only weapons we possessed were pen and ink, after all!

Some oral traditions also maintain that the Kayasth forefathers were foreigners who came to India with the Shak rulers. The Indo-Scythian satraps, contemporaries of the Kushan dynasty (c. first to third centuries CE), had their capital around Mathura, one of the places of origin of the Mathurs, the sub-caste of the Kayasths to which the LCs belong.

The office of the scribe in ancient Indian courts may have been open to people from the first three twice-born varnas and drawn from the ranks of the literate. But it was only in medieval India, with the establishment of Islamic rule in Delhi, that Kayasths seem to have made an appearance as a distinct literate community with a unique culture of amalgamation that sets them apart from the rest of the Hindu society in India. According to some historians, the word 'Kayasth', first appears in the *Akbarnama*, the biography of the Mughal emperor Akbar (r. 1556–1605). In contrast, in the *Baburnama*, the biography of Akbar's grandfather Babur (r. 1526–1530), who is regarded as the founder of the Mughal empire in India, there appears to be no mention of the term at all. It is possibly this fact that has led to the other widespread conjecture that the Kayasths emerged as a separate community during Mughal India and that Raja Todar Mal, Akbar's revenue officer, was the first Kayasth. (Some stories also suggest that Birbal, born a Brahmin, was actually the first Kayasth.)

This may not be as far-fetched as it seems. Historians agree that Akbar, influenced by the Sufi idea of *sulh-i-kul* (for the general good), fashioned a policy of social and religious tolerance that was to underpin his great empire. It was because of his liberal views of religion, which manifested in the separation of religion from the state, the setting up of civil courts that did not discriminate against non-Muslims, the abolishing of the *jizya* (the tax on non-Muslims) and the invitations to Rajputs and other Hindus to take up high administrative posts, that he was able to build – and administer – a huge empire, spanning all of north and west India and parts of the Deccan. For a Muslim ruler governing a Hindu majority, such a policy of integration was a masterstroke, enabling him to establish a stable empire. It broke away from the conventions of kingship prevalent in the subcontinent until then, where religion, politics and policy had invariably gone hand in hand. By freeing his administrative policies from the opinions and interpretations of strict clerics, Akbar paved the way for a more modern, syncretic 'India', maintaining its pluralistic character while bringing the different strands together. It can be said that almost 500 years before the Constitution of a free nation finally enshrined these values, they became part of our consciousness as a people. And Kayasths were, possibly, the first by-products of this change.

The story that Todar Mal or Birbal was a Kayasth probably arose because of this political–cultural climate where, for the first time in the subcontinent's history, Hindus and Muslims interacted very closely both in the social and professional spheres. The community of scribes, educated in Persian, may have become inseparable not just from the outer political world of the Muslim courts but also from the inner world of the emperors and their confidants. Amicable social bonds, sometimes even bonds of friendship, may have been formed at least between the menfolk interacting in public domains. Food and wine may have been shared to deepen these bonds, and a separate Kayasth culture – as also 'caste' – much closer in its way of living to the dominant Mughal lifestyle than to the rest of the population of Hindustan came into existence. Kayasth cuisine, the community's fondness for liquor, its speech, sartorial style, formal, urbane manners, pursuit of music and *shayari* all seem to support this Indo-Islamic genesis.

Another interesting theory about the origin of the community is postulated in a book called *Aquam-al-Hind*, published in the early twentieth century. According to this hypothesis, Kayasths can trace their ancestry to the graduates of a school teaching Arabic and Persian established by Sikander Lodi (r. 1489–1517) in Agra to generate literate manpower to be used as accountants and clerks – *munshis* – in the Lodi state. Young men from various local Hindu communities of northern India enrolled here in the hope of eventually gaining employment. As they grew to learn the language of power and find employment, they gradually absorbed the dominant Islamic culture of the day. In fact, it is suggested that the word 'Kayasth' can be traced to the Persian word *katib*, literally 'writer'.

This theory seems credible too, considering the Kayasths, besides being part of the Mughal courts in Agra and old Delhi (and later Lucknow and other principalities), were also based in villages and small towns in the Indo-Gangetic plain, where they were custodians of land records. Many of them were designated as lekhpal, patwari, munshi and kanungo – in district gazetteers for keepers of handwritten records of ownership. Much of the legalese in these records was (and continues to be) in Persian though the records themselves began to be written in Urdu.

As people well versed in the language of power and in government functioning, Kayasth scribes became powerful, managing to not just make a living by the might of the pen but also by acquiring some land, even though they were not traditionally landowners. Some who functioned in the revenue services were awarded land by both the Mughals and the British in rural areas, particularly in eastern UP, and conferred zamindari titles by the British. In UP these Kayasth scribes were typically called 'lala', attesting to their well-to-do, commanding status in the village hierarchy; sometimes they would be – perhaps inevitable for those in power – exploitative as well.

The theory that young graduates from *different* Hindu communities (not just one) were the forefathers of the Kayasths is interesting because it explains why different Kayasth sub-castes are culturally closer to certain castes like the trade-oriented baniyas, while others are more akin to the Rajput kshatriyas. While the larger Kayasth culture may be similar, there are differences in lifestyle, customs and certainly food between the various sub-castes. Kayasth sub-castes can be identified by their surnames. In UP and Bihar, these would be Mathur, Srivastava, Saxena, Asthana and so on, though an inordinately large number don't have the caste suffixes in their names, using caste-neutral variants like Sahay, Chandra, Saharia and Kumar. The non-use of caste surnames, however, does not preclude the formation of an egalitarian world. Most Kayasth families do not see their distinct culture as being a part of a larger confluence of cultures and, in fact, firmly entrenched rivalries exist between different sub-castes. The distinctions between them have, over the years, spawned games of one-upmanship, snobbery wars and a new social hierarchy within the larger community.

Barima, for instance, was convinced that the Mathurs were the most superior species on the planet, a notch above the Saxenas, Srivastavas and Asthanas. For her, it was the UP Kayasth families that were inherently virtuous. In her failed bid at groom hunting for me, the criterion was clear: the boy must be from a pedigreed UP family, from Lucknow or Agra, or even Bareilly, Meerut or Kanpur. Abbaji, her father, had 'given away' one of his three daughters to a Rajasthani (Mathur) family, and while Barima was full of admiration for the gentle brother-in-law and her sister's whole-hearted adaptation to the Rajput-influenced way of life, she would always let out a tiny shudder at the thought of the *ghunghat* and *bodla* and *hukum*, broad culture stereotypes connoting a cloistered existence for women, that defined her sister's life after marriage. The Kayasths of Rajasthan, many of whom had migrated from UP and Delhi to serve with the princely states after the decline of the Mughal courts, have usually been regarded as far more provincial than the UP or Delhi Kayasths. Their mores were influenced by the Rajput way of living and neither their prowess when it came to cooking raan (a whole leg of lamb, a Rajput speciality) nor their easy access to churan, supari or gota (mouth fresheners with fennel, dry coconut flakes and much else, the best varieties of which are usually found in Rajasthani homes) could convince Barima to view their culture as a desirable one.

Whether it was in Bihar, MP or Patiala in Punjab (and at one time Lahore, now in Pakistan), Kayasth *garhs*, centres, in other parts of the country did not even penetrate our consciousness. The Dilli-wallas were regarded as being in a different league altogether. The Kayasths here, and more specifically the Mathurs of Shahar – the city – as old Delhi Mathurs called their city with pride, with most older affluent families settling in Civil Lines – had always considered themselves to be culturally one up on the rest. But UP families like that of the LCs were dismissive of that claim and looked upon Delhi families as a little too 'fast', slightly Machiavellian, more given to show and ostentation with their khana–peena and rituals, compared to the sober and straight-forward UP-wallas.

For instance, the Dilli-wallas have the more showy *mehndi* as part of their wedding rituals – an evening of not just applying the auspicious henna on the palms of the bride and the groom, but music, dancing, drinking and partaking of food sent by the girl's family to the boy's. In contrast, the UP-wallas have the sedate saya sagai, an engagement ritual in lieu of the *mehndi*, on the evening before the main wedding ceremony. Both rituals have their moorings in Mughal culture. Mehndi is a ritual followed in many Muslim weddings in the subcontinent, and saya sagai is a ritual involving an elaborate formal invitation to the groom's family to come to the girl's home the next day with the *baraat*, the marriage procession. The letter that accompanies the sweets and snacks is written in flowery Urdu, sometimes extending to several pages as Mathur Kayasths let their passion for home-made verse, and not just home-made food, flow. Both the poetry and the food derive from the Indo-Islamic world that gave birth to the community.

3

The Ganga–Jamuni Fusion

Of Identity and Food

Rai Mahimapat Ray, 'Ray' to friends, part of the elite IAS and belonging to a prominent landed Srivastava family from eastern UP, gets a trifle riled when I ask him about the Kayasth cuisine of his family. Especially the cooking of his nani, his maternal grandmother, who belonged to one of the oldest Kayasth families in Lucknow, settled in Ghasiyari Mandi.

Like my own memories of all the deliciousness on Barima's table, Ray has vivid ones of his nani cooking: the way her tehri would be suffused with the flavours of *khada*, whole, garam masala, and the kaliya she cooked, whose pleasure lay as much in the texture and flavour of the potato or fried colocasia, added to the thin gravy as in the well-doneness of the goat meat. He remembers the kachche keema ke kofte she would fashion in a jiffy for an afternoon meal, as also the atte ka keema, a faux non-vegetarian dish that took hours of preparation as she painstakingly washed the starch off the wheat dough till only the insoluble, spongy gluten remained. But despite waxing eloquent on all of this, Ray is uncomfortable with the tag 'Kayasth cuisine'.

'No one should talk about caste in modern India,' he says, sounding irritated.

As a young, globalized, Indian, Ray is right. Despite its politicization and the fact that both work and education opportunities for many in the country are dependent on their caste, for many Hindus privileged enough to have escaped its ramifications through education, wealth, enterprise or private-sector jobs, caste has become somewhat irrelevant. That is India's strange reality.

It is class that may be more pertinent to urban lifestyles. Which restaurants, bars and cafes does one go to? How often does one travel abroad, for work or leisure? Which modern service behemoth does one draw one's salary from or which knowledge-based start-up does one aspire to be employed with? Where one lives, which school one attended, whether one can speak English well – that arbitrator of social status in India – and where one last holidayed are perhaps factors that distinguish us more, socially, than which community we were born into or what our ancestors did.

Indeed, for those who grew up in a 'liberalized' world and who attended the best private schools in the country, why should caste matter? Many of our parents and grandparents – the 1970s' Bachchan-era rebels, the idealists of the Independence movement – seem to have moved beyond caste as a denominator. So why must our generation and the ones following look at our lives and culture through that prism today? Isn't that regressive? In a society fractured along so many fault lines, should food not bind instead of being the mark for separate identities?

It is an argument I am happy to make. Except that it would be impossible to refer to cuisine and culinary traditions in India without reference to caste. Not only do food and traditions of cooking and eating change in the country every few hundred kilometres, but they also change from home to home; indeed, flavours depend on which 'hand' has added the masala. Fold a banana leaf, on which you have eaten, one way, and you signal your 'higher' caste; do it the opposite way and your social pedigree is automatically lowered. These are practices that still exist in a complex country at once 'modern' and ancient, and to document any cuisine and examine it in the context of a larger culture requires caste to be brought firmly centre stage. However much we may like to escape tags, however much we aspire to globalized palates and lives, the study of traditional cuisines and practices in India, like anywhere else in the world, must necessarily involve a close study of often self-contained, homogeneous and exclusivist communities.

If Ray is uncomfortable with the thought of caste entering our discussions on food, he is hardly alone. Kayasth families, over generations, seem to have displayed remarkable unease at such categorizations. Caste and the Kayasths have always had an uneasy relationship. On the one hand, families like that of the LCs took pride in being more open and cosmopolitan in their adaptability to different cultural and culinary influences and consciously tried very hard not to be seen as parochial. On the other hand, the very fact that this 'urbaneness' was worn as a badge to set the Kayasths apart as a distinctive, exclusive community made theirs a relatively narrow, self-contained world.

The Kayasth elders of my grandparents' generation whom I have had the privilege of knowing, took great pride in their education and 'culture' – in the impeccable crisp whiteness of the starched kurta–pyjamas (the Muslim dress, not the dhoti–kurta of other Hindu families) they wore, as also achkans (long, high-collared coats worn for formal occasions); in their proficiency in sher-o-shayari and Hindustani classical music; and in their British-influenced dining tables, porcelain tea sets, baking skills and their prowess in speaking and writing English. Quotes from Chaucer, Milton or Shakespeare rolled off their tongues as easily as self-composed Urdu verse and dohas from the Ramayana. In other words, they were cultured, *shaukeen* folk. There is no English word that conveys the nuances of the word shaukeen. 'Connoisseur' is close to the spirit of it, though 'pleasure pursuer' or 'one who follows his hobbies' would be a more literal translation. Both these translations, however, lack the gravitas and courtliness associated with a true shaukeen.

Ironically, in seeing themselves as distinct, Kayasths have reinforced their caste credentials. It is a complex self-view, a dichotomy that I have always found fascinating.

My grandparents, Mr and Mrs LC, personified this split, dichotonomous world of the Kayasths. Lakshmi Chandra was looked up to by everyone in his family and among his peers for his 'artistic' ways. He wrote poetry, scripted plays, took an interest in cooking and in the way his table and living room looked, with their flower arrangements and pretty curtains. In short, he was an old-fashioned aesthete. He would correct me on my Urdu pronunciations, write beautiful Hindustani lyrics for songs to be sung at family weddings and functions and, at other times, pepper his speech with lines from Shakespeare and Milton. They could be inadvertently inappropriate, but to my teenage mind they opened up an alien world far removed from the provinciality of Lucknow. 'It is better to reign in Hell, than serve in Heaven' was Papa's oft-repeated homily, doled out to anyone in the family bent on taking a risky venture, which included jumping jobs, moving cities, starting businesses and other life events of a similar nature. It is quite another matter that my grandfather meant it more as a validation of risk-taking entrepreneurial zeal that he believed few Kayasths to possess naturally, than an affirmation of Milton's world view in the poem, where it is Satan who speaks his mind thus to justify his anti-establishment rebellion!

Regardless of how he interpreted *Paradise Lost*, my grandfather dreaded provinciality. Early in life, perhaps in response to the Nehruvian nationalistic fervour in

Allahabad, where he was educated in the 1930s and 1940s, he had decided to do away with caste appellations. When my father, his eldest child, was born in 1948, a year after Independence, LC took the radical step of deleting his caste from the surname. Instead, he took two first names and joined them to name my father 'Rajeev Rishi'. When my uncles were born, the new family surname had become 'Rishi'. But when my aunt, the daughter, came along, she got special treatment. 'Vishalakshi' (a name for the mother goddess in Banaras) became her surname. Decades later, I was bestowed with the same surname to keep the family tradition alive and kicking. So we became a unique, mixed family of Mathurs, Rishis and Vishalakshis – the last abbreviated to Vishal. But the eagerness to shed caste tags was superficial in many ways. Like so many Kayasth families of their milieu, mine lived in dread of intermarriages, of the pristine Kayasth-only pedigree being diluted. We could have mixed-up names and mixed-up menus, but not mixed-up bloodlines.

Many years later, when I married a non-believing half-Muslim, amongst my family's many illogical concerns was this: 'But you will be called Mrs Ahmad now.' The argument that my own surname is a made-up one, hardly the carrier of caste identity, was of no merit. To shed the caste surname may have been a symbol of 'modernity' for my family. But to actually go beyond that symbolism was not the done thing in the exclusive world of the community.

It is for this reason that I have always seen Kayasth society as Janus-faced: looking forward and backward at the same time. Stuck to some notions of roots while trying to uproot itself to a socially and materially better, more 'modern' reality. Having imbibed bits and pieces of everyone else's culture and lifestyle, the community is cosmopolitan. But in being fiercely protective of this turf, of this unique Ganga–Jamuni–colonial culture, as also its religious moorings (Kayasths retained their religion despite changing their food habits, customs and language to blend in with the ruling communities of the day, whether the Mughals or the British), in trying to maintain 'pure' bloodlines and exclusivist family structures, the community also lives in a strange, complex denial of the very melting pot that has given rise to it.

The melting pot becomes strikingly obvious in matters of food. Pasanda, kofta, kaliya, shami kebab – all the big-ticket meat dishes in the Kayasth repertoire undoubtedly bear a Mughal/Nawabi influence. Thanks to the proximity of the community to Muslim nobility, the preference for red meat became as much a part of Kayasth lifestyle and home-cooking as in Muslim homes. So firmly was non-vegetarianism embedded in the food habits of the community that most affluent families had at least one meat dish on the table for dinner – very different from the custom of other 'upper-caste' Hindu communities of the time. In fact, dishes like the kaliya found exalted, almost ritualistic status. In the home of the LCs, and indeed in other Kayasth homes, to cook meat was symbolic of a happy and auspicious time.

Festive or celebratory occasions generally saw the appearance of richer and more sumptuous non-vegetarian food on the table, usually paired with pooris. Snacks like shami kebabs or fried kofte, preferred with chotta pegs of whisky and sundowners as the Kayasths took on colonial customs, could still be eaten by themselves at tea, but a heartier main meal would see even these paired with fried carbs. A popular combination was shami kebabs with pan-fried parathas, made almost daily at home for at least one meal. Kebab–parathas worked as a breakfast dish, as a filling evening supper or as a picnicky snack. I liked the last the best. The flat kebab would be wrapped in the distinctive triangular paratha of Kayasth homes and we would happily munch on them in the car or train while travelling, or during picnics with food spread out on durries.

This pairing, in Kayasth homes, of fried breads – regarded as celebratory and ritualistically superior food – with the kind of non-vegetarian dishes favoured by the Muslim elite, is one of the most startling and visible examples of the confluence of Indo and Islamic cultures in northern India. Kebab–paratha is a common snack of Muslim homes in the Hindi heartland as also in Pakistan's Punjab. To most people in the Indian subcontinent, poori–aloo – the potatoes being done in different styles and with different spices in different regions – is a classic, popular and satiating combination.

khana. Anything cooked without ghee was kachcha khana, inferior, not to be stored if made during the day. In most 'upper-caste' homes, whether Baniya, Brahmin or Kshatriya – not to mention Kayasth – paratha (pakka khana) was the main bread eaten during the evening meal, in contrast to the roti or phulka cooked on the tawa without ghee (kachcha khana) that could be eaten for lunch. Kachcha khana was also what was cooked and eaten in times of mourning – dal without tempering, vegetables without turmeric, the other 'purifying' ingredient in Hindu cooking and breads made without frying. Pakka khana (such as pooris, fried and puffed in the kadhai), on the other hand, was a must during celebrations and festivities. Though ritualistic feasts, cooked in temples and offered as prasad could be both *pakki rasoi* (poori–aloo, kheer or rice pudding and vegetables like pumpkin cooked without onion and garlic) or *kachchi rasoi* (kadhi–chawal, aloo, pumpkin), food that had been cooked in oil and thus sanctified was considered to be superior. It is because of such a classification of food that *kadhai chadana*, or frying the ingredients in ghee in the wok, became a ritual in itself, whether you were making a halwa for a puja or frying pooris.

Although 'outsiders', or non-Kayasths, have always seen Kayasths as 'adhe Mussalman' or half Muslim, within the community, and in the LCs' home for sure, there seemed to exist a great suspicion of the 'other'. For the longest time, Barima did not want to eat out in restaurants where she suspected the cook could be Muslim. She was not unique in this. It was a common way of thinking, especially for vegetarian Kayasth women who did not usually interact outside religious boundaries. Paradoxically, Mrs LC would be upset if she found that meat had not been cooked on a festive day. Like the ritualistic use of ghee, cooking meat too signified plenty. It was eschewed during times of mourning or abstaining and cooked when you needed to signal the resuming of a 'full life'.

In caste-ridden Hindu society, different types of meats were traditionally prescribed for different communities. According to some historians, while Vedic texts mention beef being part of the Aryan diet, especially in the aftermath of sacred sacrifices, the Kshatriyas, who were warriors, certainly ate game. Flavourful venison was prescribed for the royals. Versions of the Ramayana mention Sita, a deity along with Ram to millions of Indians, longing for deer meat while exiled in the forest, according to the redoubtable K.T. Achaya who has researched Indian food history in such depth. It was with the reformist spirit of Buddhism and Jainism, as monastic orders were established that rituals, sacrifices and meat eating in ancient India took a back seat. Hinduism changed as a reaction to the emergence of these new religions and a more frugal sense of piety took over. Meat eating began to be socially and religiously shunned by the three 'upper' castes of Hindu society while those designated as 'lower-castes' continued with their cheaper sources of protein and sustenance. All this is fairly common knowledge.

The Kayasths, never part of the strict Vedic caste hierarchy, a made-up community of fused identities, looked at meat eating quite differently. The original strain of 'upper-caste' Hindu more, dominant within the community in many ways, may have frowned upon non-vegetarianism, viewing it as 'unclean' and ritualistically impure, but with the new rulers from Central Asia firmly ensconced, meat eating became acceptable.

The Rajputs, a community in India that ostensibly traces its origins to the warrior Kshatriyas and which also seems to have sprung up in the subcontinent in medieval times, eat meat as well. For them meat is a symbol of royalty, power and plenty. The Kayasths, affluent by association with the new powerful elite of the subcontinent, the Mughal rulers, treated non-vegetarianism in a similar way. They imbibed the courtly traditions and dishes, and turned these into rituals of prosperity and plenty. In the melting pot of the subcontinent, as new identities were forged, new food traditions came up. The food culture of the Kayasths is a reflection of the heterogenous identity of the community, assimilating different influences over a period of perhaps a thousand years. The Kayasths may or may not have been 'tolerant', but their cuisine has to be one of India's most 'tolerant' foods.

PART II

ON MRS LC's TABLE

As one of India's foremost examples of 'fusion' food, the Ganga–Jamuni cuisine of the Kayasths relied on fresh local and seasonal ingredients that varied according to the region to which the community spread. Summer meant the arrival of vegetables like karela, tinda, torai and bhindi on the table, as also fruits like mango. The LCs, thanks to their Moradabad roots, preferred the langda over the sweeter dussehri. The Railways bungalows they were allotted would usually have a few mango trees. *Daal ke aam*, mangoes that had ripened on the branches, were infinitely preferable to *paal ke aam*, those ripened indoors. Invariably, one room in the house was reserved for ripening mangoes in bulk, their scent filling up the long summers. The extended family would gather for mango parties in the evenings, picking out fruits cooling in buckets of water – usually the small *chusiya*, suckable, variety – and devour half a dozen or more per person.

Winters, on the other hand, spelt guavas, the best of which, the ones from Allahabad, inspired poetic verses in the family. The season also brought with it an exciting choice of vegetables for cooking – bathua, patta gobhi, shalgam, methi and gajar. Many of these were cooked with meat. Shabdeg, a preparation in which turnips and meat are stewed overnight on a slow fire, was a delicacy, a much rarer occurrance than the home-style kaliya, kofte and even pasande that formed the holy trinity of our home food. It was a dish for feasts, for large, special-occasion meals cooked by Muslim *bawarchis*, cooks patronized by the Kayasth families in Lucknow or Delhi.

The spices that went into each of the preparations also varied according to the seasons. In summer, in the UP family home of the LCs, amchoor, or dried mango, reigned supreme, along with crushed fennel seeds, both cooling spices. Amchoor was used in arhar dal, or yellow pigeon pea, and in dry spice mixtures assembled in-house to make bharwan dishes – stuffed bhindi, karela and other vegetables. Winters meant a heavier use of cloves, peeli mirch or yellow chilli powder, and garlic, a warming ingredient. But most of the spice 'combinations' were almost instinctive. Without any recorded recipes, or even without being expressly taught, we knew which spices to use with each ingredient. This knowledge had got passed down through generations, as in most Indian kitchens, and even today if I look at baigan, I automatically reach for kalonji (onion seeds), which my family uses to flavour a dry preparation. Similarly, I have an inherent disdain for anyone using zeera, cumin, in an onion–garlic masala. Along with heeng, or asafoetida, zeera was only used in 'pure vegetarian', no-onion cooking. I can now analyse that the sulphur-rich flavour profile of the spices perhaps approximates the taste of onions, and hence there is no point in using these spices in an onion-based gravy. But cooks instinctively followed these patterns of spicing without giving much thought to the reasons behind their choices.

The lentil, an overwhelmingly important ingredient in the Kayasth kitchen, was also used to whip up mock meats, dishes invented to approximate the flavours and textures of popular meat dishes. This seems to be a uniquely Kayasth strand of cooking. The type of dal we ate also changed according to seasons. Arhar was the undisputed summer king and split (husk-less) urad, or white lentils, was used to make richer winter preparations; moong was used to make fritters across seasons as well as dumplings that could be curried.

Dum, steam-cooking, or letting food cook in its own juices in sealed containers over a slow fire, was an important cooking technique. Bhuna was equally vital in Kayasth homes. The idea was to cook meats or even green vegetables slowly and well so that the flavours got concentrated as water evaporated. 'Bhun-na', or the technique of 'bhunoing', as I have referred to it in this book, does not have an English equivalent. Saute or stir-fry do not convey its essence. In the Kayasth kitchen, properly bhunoing an onion masala was the basic first step to a good curry, for instance. Slowly browning the grated onions, adding small quantities of yoghurt at intervals to add acidity and fat, was a laborious task. You had to keep stirring the onions and ensure that they were properly browned but not burnt. Once the oil was released and came to float on top, the dry spices could be added before bhunoing for a few more minutes. Only then was water added to complete the cooking. The resulting masala, enhanced with other dry spices, could be a base for many preparations. But, for Mrs LC, the masala itself worked as a substitute for the main dish itself.

One of my many memories of Barima at the dining table is of her asking for just some bhuna onion masala with parathas for dinner. As we know, she could be extraordinarily picky, and she would resort to this demand on days when nothing else that was being cooked appealed to her. But those days were rare. Mrs LC's table always had huge amounts of food to cater to almost any palate, and unexpected guests too. From lentils imaginatively cooked, or at least properly tempered with the correct combination of spices, to at least two bhuna or bharwan vegetarian dishes, to a meat curry or meat kofte, seasonal pickles, chutneys and parathas, the table was always full.

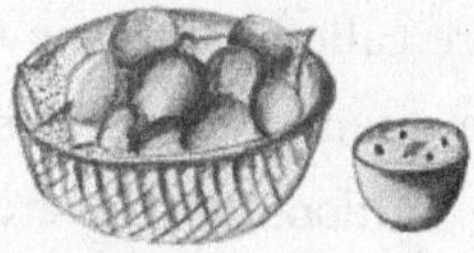

4

No Dull Days with Dal

How Lentils Turn into Kebab and Kaleji

If there is one dish that springs to my mind while thinking of Barima, it is undoubtedly pakori ki subzi – split moong dal dumplings in a gravy. It was her favourite, and at least once a week, she would have it with crisp parathas for dinner, often feeding us, her grandchildren, little bites from her plate. It is the texture of the pakori that has stayed on with me – so soft that a touch of the spoon would split it. Flavoured with asafoetida and soaked in a light curry, the pakori was the perfect foil to flaky bread.

The lentil dumpling is one of the most common Indian snacks. One can argue that it travelled from the Turkish/ Mediterranean region to the subcontinent. The falafel is certainly a cousin of the Indian pakori, with the abundantly available moong beans in the country replacing the fava. In Delhi, these fritters are a popular street snack in winter. Even today, when so much of the old city and its culture has perished, Ram laddoos, as they are called, continue to be hawked by vendors who take their cane baskets from one locality to another, garnishing the 'laddoos' with grated radish and serving it up with the tart coriander chutney typical of this region.

The same pakori is served in a favoured chaat item in UP, dahi ki pakori, in which the pakoris are dunked in yoghurt with dollops of saunth (tamarind sauce) and sprinkled with dry roasted zeera powder, salt and red chilli powder, the most basic of home-style chaat masalas. The dahi bada, of course, is a cousin of the dahi pakori, as is the dahi gujiya, variations of the same basic lentil fritter popular across northern India and across religious communities as well. (The dahi pakori, or dahi phulki as they are called in Muslim homes, is an old Delhi/UP iftar snack, for instance.) As we travel further down the length of the subcontinent, the pakori changes character – bits of spices get added. The mangore of Madhya Pradesh are flavoured with robust whole, pounded coriander seeds. Further south stronger flavours come in to play and other lentils are used. The medhu vada, for instance, is made with urad dal which is more starchy and transforms into a different snack altogether.

In spite of the many avataars it assumes hardly ever is the humble pakori prepared and eaten as an exquisite main course dish with such subtlety as in Kayasth homes. You could make a light onion gravy for the small, soft pakoris (without tomatoes, a much later entrant into north Indian kitchens), but the way Barima ate this dish was in an even more pristine form: a watery soup-like gravy flavoured with asafoetida, turmeric, coriander powder and lots of chopped green coriander became the mother ocean in which the perfectly fried, crunchy golden rounds of lentil floated. No baking powder or soda was used to ensure the fluffiness of the fritters. It was just the way you beat the ground dal with your hand, aerating it, that did the trick – and it was a dexterous trick. Pakori ki subzi may look deceptively easy to cook, but it is a dish that has great potential to go wrong in the kitchen if the lightness or deftness of touch is missing. It takes a skilled cook indeed to ensure the perfectly soft texture of the fritters, a skill that has entirely bypassed most street vendors who go about selling Ram Laddoos.

Being Barima's favourite ingredient, the humble moong found itself transformed into many such exotic forms in her kitchen, to be served as breakfast specials and tea-time or whisky-time snacks. A popular snack at breakfast or other times was chunki, or moong dal sautéed in a little hot oil to which a touch of asafoetida had been added and then steamed in just a little water, so that it stayed a dry dish. It could be topped with lemon and ginger slivers and perhaps some finely chopped green chillies for a satisfying protein burst that could keep you going for hours.

This method of cooking a lentil is quite different from how dals are usually prepared. Lentils are first boiled in water to the required consistency (thick, slushy arhar, dry urad or watery moong) and then tempered with appropriate spices – heeng, zeera and whole red chillies for arhar; heeng with the occasional addition of garlic for dry urad; and heeng, ginger and sometimes shah zeera for moong. The shah zeera is darker and sweeter than regular cumin, and its aroma when it is toasted is nuttier. Each dal has its own set of tempering ingredients to be used in different combinations. This is very difficult to explain it to a public habituated to the generic onion–garlic–tomato–red chilli tadka of 'north Indian' khana, or at least, the Punjabi-dominated restaurant cooking that now defines our palates and kitchen practices.

In any case, chunki moong, the breakfast dish, is what has mutated into the Dal Moradabadi that restaurants serve today. But while that dal was indeed a commonly available snack in Moradabad, what made it to the bazaar was a spiced and chutneyed-up form. Like most Kayasth families, we did not add the ubiquitous garam masala, literally 'hot' or heat-inducing spices, to the light snack. Nor did we sprinkle, as a post-cooking condiment, any chaat masala, the mixture of spices with a hot and sour flavour profile that is easily available as a packaged single entity today and liberally used both in homes and commercial cooking. Both these additions perhaps occurred when the snack made it to the bazaars. To be an everyman dish, the flavours needed to be bolder and nothing could be easier in achieving this than adding a pinch or more of garam masala and/or chaat masala plus a dash of tangy coriander chutney (commonly used to garnish chaat in UP) to the steamed lentils. But like sushi-dunked-in-soy, where what you are really tasting is the saltiness of the soy sauce (this way of slathering the delicate and nuanced flavours with a strong condiment may be one reason why so many people in India love sushi), dal dunked in chaat-style condiments masks its basic flavour, especially when it comes to a grain as delicate as the moong.

Here, Chef Manish Mehrotra's rendition of Dal Moradabadi in the celebrated restaurant, Indian Accent, in Delhi, the mecca of contemporary Indian cuisine, warrants mention. It is one of my favourite restaurant dishes of all time. In the hands of a talented, sophisticated chef like Mehrotra the Kayasth chunki moong assumes a different avatar, transforming into a haute food item. It loses some of its all-you-can-dunk-it-in bazaar sensibility. Mehrotra cleans up the original dish by adding into it a few cloves instead of garam masala, giving it a distinct flavour profile. And it is served beautifully, accompanied by small portions of fried onions (not the raw, finely chopped onion we sprinkled over it at Mrs LC's table), lime, chaat masala and kurkure (the Indian version of crisps), which add some more flavours and textures. I have to admit I prefer Chef Mehrotra's playful version to Mrs LC's more pristine one because, after all, unlike my classic grandmother, my tastes often run towards the more kitschy.

The moong regularly found its way to Mrs LC's table masqueraded as many other things, in a variety of forms that were difficult to resist. There were moong dal chilas that my grandmother was partial to and so these were breakfast staples in winter. Then, there were her gorgeous moong dal shami kebabs, her skill in crafting these at par with her dexterity in making the 'real' meat kebabs. Much before the advent of restaurateurs who introduced vegetarian kebabs of all kinds to cater to vegetarian folk looking for more exotic fare than home-style food, such innovations were the norm in Kayasth homes. Long before the onslaught of the 'veg galauti – so real that you can barely tell the difference', we already had our moong dal shami kebabs, moong dal kofte and even our version of the kaleji made, but of course, from moong dal! But we shall talk about these delicacies in the following chapter.

While moong dal was a favoured ingredient for many dishes on Mrs LC's table, it wasn't as if the family loved – or even *liked* – this dal per se. As a child, I detested moong dal. I looked at moong dal khichdi as a dish fit only for the ill and the stricken, and it is perhaps the only food I would never voluntarily consume in times of good health and cheer. I was remarkably non-fussy otherwise, eating all my greens as well as the treats at the table. Luckily, plain moong dal was hardly ever prepared in our home. Even in winter, when in-season spinach meant that you could make a far more fetching concoction, seasoning the lentil with sautéed spinach leaves, ginger juliennes and green chillies, there were relatively few days when we had moong dal as simply *dal*.

Arhar dal, the staple of UP and Bihar, was the overwhelming favourite with everyone and most of our meals would feature a nicely tempered version of it. My father would especially enter the kitchen just before dinner to put his trademark strong *chownk*, tempering, of heeng, zeera and sabut lal mirch in desi ghee – it made for a very flavourful thick dal. In summer, my mother would boil arhar with a piece of kairi, or raw mango, and we would have a tangier concoction, alive with the flavours of the season, mint and mango. At these lunches, my grandfather would invariably get into his 'food' storytelling mood, fondly recalling meals consumed while he was posted in Chandausi or elsewhere in the boondocks, when rustic cooks would cook the dal in earthenware on the embers of a wood-fired chulha in the courtyard. Rotis would be made on this makeshift mud oven too, the smoky flavour from the burning wood pepping up the humble meal. My family, which had become urbanized fairly early in its history and which thrived on modern conveniences like refrigerators and LPG fuel (just making their entrance into middle-class homes in the 1950s), still clung to this nostalgia for a more earthy existence. Smoked arhar dal with raw mango was a food memory to fall back on for comfort.

But the dal of choice while entertaining in those days was definitely urad. Sabut or black urad – the mah ki dal of Punjabi homes or the popular dal makhani of restaurants – being reviled by the LC family and cooked only during times of mourning and tragedy, its husk-less white cousin, dhuli urad, despite being a heavier grain to digest, was not only a regular part of home meals but almost the only lentil served at dinner parties, feasts and festivals. Eating in

Kayasth households certainly was – and still is – a nuanced affair! Sookhi urad is, in fact, quite a Kayasth speciality, the split dal cooked with just enough water to leave the grains separate and dry. It is served with a garnish of fried onions and a tempering of red whole chillies and asafoetida in ghee. No cumin seeds are used in the chownk, unlike for other liquid dal preparations. Sookhi urad has occupied its pride of place on the family table ever since the time of my great-grandfather, Pradyumn Krishna Mathur. Legend has it that, every day, he sat in his great armchair outside his mansion in Deputy Ganj, Moradabad, fit as a fiddle at ninety, with two sacks – one of urad dal and the other of Basmati rice – at his feet. To every person who came calling, a fistful of each was donated as some sort of regal blessing, distribution of largesse by a member of a community that had made it as administrators, courtiers and landowners, and acquired befitting princely manners to go with these social positions.

Close to centres of powers in princely states or smaller districts, Kayasth men were purveyors of all the nineteenth-century aristocratic pleasures that defined high life in those times. Despite the decline of the Mughal empire and the establishment of a newer colonial order and despite the fact that Mughal decadence was giving way to Victorian morality and mores, the larger Kayasth culture remained fairly Ganga–Jamuni, with the older culture of the Muslim courts defining life and lifestyle. Men went on shikar, entertained themselves with music, dance and poetry, sometimes even wrote nazms and ghazals, dressed in kurta–pyjamas and were of a fairly shaukeen disposition in general.

Pradyumn Krishna was a shaukeen for sure, his death epitomizing that particular blend of leisure and stateliness that defined the term. When he passed on peacefully in his sleep just a few years short of a century, there was still an uneaten bida of paan stowed away in his cheek. He must have got up during the night, prepared a Banarsi paan for himself just the way he liked, layering the betel leaf methodically with condiments such as chuna, katha, gulukand and adding a supari (areca nut, neatly broken down into small pellets). Chewing on the betel leaf was his habit – like all shaukeen men of his day, he was hardly ever without the tell-tale red stain on his lips and teeth – and he was not about to leave this world without his favourite stimulant. The paan remained unchewed, tucked into his mouth, as he passed on – gently, gloriously, like a king, not because of any lingering illness but because his heart stopped beating. Every day, till his death, Pradyumn Krishna maintained his robust diet of a lunch of a couple of karari roti with a bowl of *sookhi* (dry) urad dal that floated in almost an equal quantity of ghee. That was his only meal in the day, and his digestion was none the worse for the heavy lentils he partook of.

Apart from the dry version, split urad was sometimes slow-cooked with winter greens like methi till they had blended perfectly and you couldn't distinguish the grain from the green. This preparation, called satpaita, was another favourite on Mrs LC's table.

Recipes

Sookhi Urad Dal

There are two versions of this dry dal, depending on the quantity of water used to boil it. The recipe given here is for the 'khilwa' dal, which uses just enough water to keep the grains separate. The 'laddoo' dal preferred by my great-grandfather Pradyumn Krishna, on the other hand, is mashed up. For this, a depression is made in the centre of the mashed dal into which pyaaz ka ghee, ghee in which onions have been browned so that it retains the fried onion flavour, is generously poured.

Serves 4

INGREDIENTS

- 500g split and skinless urad dal, washed
- ½ tsp turmeric powder
- Salt to taste
- 4 tbsp ghee
- 2 onions, thinly sliced
- 1 big pinch of asafoetida
- 4 dry red chillies

METHOD

Add turmeric and salt to the urad, and boil it in just enough water till it is cooked with the grains staying separate, about 15 minutes if cooking in a pressure cooker.

Heat the ghee in a pan and fry the sliced onions till golden brown. Remove the onions with a slotted spoon and keep aside.

In the pyaaz ka ghee, the ghee that has been flavoured while browning onions, add the asafoetida and the red chillies, and fry for 1–2 minutes.

Temper the dal with this.

Spread the browned onions on top.

Serve hot with crisp rotis.

Pakori ki Subzi

Barima's favourite, this simple curry gets its flavour from heeng or asafoetida. But you can also make a heavier onion gravy for the pakori. Garlic, however, is strictly a no-no.

Serves 4

INGREDIENTS

The pakoris

1 cup of skinless moong dal, cleaned, washed and soaked in water for at least 1 hour
3–4 green chillies, finely chopped
A pinch of asafoetida
Salt to taste
A pinch of soda bicarbonate (optional)
Oil for frying

The gravy

2 tbsp oil
A pinch of asafoetida
1 tsp turmeric powder

1 tsp coriander powder
1 tsp red chilli powder
Water for a thin curry
Salt to taste
1 tbsp coriander leaves, chopped

Method

For the pakoris (makes about 20 pakoris)

Drain the soaked dal of all extra water and grind to a coarse mixture.

Add green chillies and the heeng.

Now add the salt and beat the mixture well to aerate. (If using the pakoris in a gravy, you can make them without salt.) You could add a pinch of soda bicarbonate too.

Heat oil in a kadhai. When it is smoking hot, drop little spoons of the mixture and deep-fry till golden.

Take out the balls with a slotted spoon, drain out the extra oil on kitchen towels.

Serve hot with a coriander chutney as a snack or use to make pakori ki subzi.

For the gravy

Heat oil in a pan. Add the asafoetida and then the turmeric, coriander and red chilli powders. Stir-fry the masala for 2 minutes on a medium flame.

Add the water and bring it to a boil. Then lower the flame and let it simmer for 1–2 minutes.

Gently lower the pakoris into the curry. Let it simmer for 3–4 minutes till the pakoris absorb the heat and the curry to become a little soft.

Transfer to a serving dish. Garnish with fresh coriander leaves and serve with parathas.

Satpaita

All dals have complicated tempering rules. Typically, if using heeng, garlic is not added; only cumin seeds are used. Satpaita is an exception. No cumin is used to temper this urad dal, and both heeng and garlic are used to temper the dish.

Serves 4

INGREDIENTS

1 cup split urad dal, washed
4 glasses of water
1 tsp salt
½ tsp turmeric powder
2 tbsp desi ghee
2 tbsp ginger juliennes
1 cup methi leaves, finely chopped
A pinch of asafoetida
3 green chillies, slit
1 tsp chopped garlic

METHOD

Cook the dal in water, adding salt and turmeric powder.

Sauté the ginger and methi leaves in ghee and add these to the boiling dal.

Let it cook, approximately 15–20 minutes on a low flame, till it is all mashed and everything has blended well. Add more water if needed.

Temper with heeng, green chillies and chopped garlic.

5

Sab Naqli Hai

Faux Non-vegetarian Khana

'Can you make out the difference?' Papa would relish quizzing anyone sharing our lunch of faux *machchli*. The raw-banana 'fish' was a favourite dish on my grandparents' table. Mostly a winter afternoon staple, this delicious curried 'fillet' was eaten with arhar dal and plain aromatic Basmati rice. It was food that offered great joy to my grandparents, who were vegetarians, Barima a lifelong one and LC in his later years.

Kele ki machchli, or 'fish' fashioned from plantain, was a simple dish where the raw banana flavour was cleverly masked and the landlocked north Indian palate tricked into believing that this was indeed a home-style fish curry. The curry was flavoured with kasoori methi, or dried fenugreek leaves. The banana itself was cut lengthwise in the shape of fillets, coated with gram flour and fried till crisp. These fillets were then simmered in a thick onion and tomato gravy for just a couple of minutes so that they retained their texture while soaking up the flavours of the curry.

I have to admit it wasn't a bad approximation of the way in which most north Indian homes cook fish, masking its flavour and smell with spices and herbs, in this case the very powerfully fragrant dried fenugreek. Fenugreek and fish remains a classic north Indian combination. In all probability, kele ki machchli was a later-day invention in the home of my grandparents – either to make the humble plantain more palatable or to simply replicate non-vegetarian flavours and textures for vegetarians in the household. But such *paheli ka khana*, food that flummoxes the diner, seems to have been a tradition with Kayasth households anyway.

I first came across references to paheli ka khana in Hyderabad. Old Nizami families and upper-class Muslim homes have an entire repertoire of quirky dishes meant to trick the palates of guests through the creation of interesting culinary illusions and, in the end, elicit applause for sheer inventiveness and innovation. These dishes would often be presented as a jest. For instance, a newly married bridegroom enjoying the hospitality of his in-laws could be presented with a lukhmi, a traditional pie, as part of the meal in his honour. When poked open, the pastry shell would reveal a live quail that would fly away!

Cooks and ladies ruling the kitchens invested a considerable amount of time and talent perfecting such tricky and undoubtedly complicated sleights of hand.

Ingredients would be masked with flavouring and spicing, and made to look completely different from what they actually were. It was a style of cooking perfected in many royal kitchens of princely India where entertainment and cuisine were looked upon as art forms and enjoyed the patronage of royal and upper-class families. It was also a style of cooking completely at odds with the way in which we are increasingly looking at food today – where ingredients take centre stage and their intrinsic flavours are highlighted rather than disguised. But that is another story and quite another argument.

In Kayasth households, much like paheli ka khana, an entire strand of cooking involved dishes that were not what they seemed. Essentially, these were vegetarian dishes made to look, feel and taste like non-vegetarian dishes, like kele ki machchli, or moong dal ke shami kebab, or atte ka keema, and so on. For a community in which most of the women remained vegetarian for religious reasons even as the men adopted meat eating (and other cultural nuances) of the ruling classes, it must have been quite natural to experiment and come up with vegetarian alternatives to popular non-vegetarian dishes. What is interesting is that never having tasted meat at all, Kayasth women were still able to replicate quite dexterously, fairly authentic meaty flavours from humble ingredients in their kitchen.

Barima, for instance, despite never having tasted liver, was adept at making kaleji ki subzi – false liver. (My family, in any case, has been quite the exception amongst the clan for eschewing the typical bhuna gurda kaleji favoured in other Kayasth homes.) Soaked and ground moong dal would be seasoned with garlic and garam masala, steamed in little muslin bags and cut into little irregular shaped dumplings. These were then cooked in a thick gravy, with the masala and texture of the nuggets evoking a masala-clad, bhuna liver preparation. Since even real liver preparations involved hiding the strong smell and taste of offal by cooking it in milk, bhunoing it over a slow fire and coating it in masala, both the end results tasted quite similar.

Raw jackfruit, regarded as the 'meat for vegetarians' because of the way it looks and because of its texture, was another ingredient commonly used in faux non-vegetarian recipes. Cooking the most tender of small jackfruits available only during the monsoon was an art in itself. In the assorted UP towns where my grandparents stayed for the duration of LC's Railways career, there was always a jackfruit tree or two either within the bungalow compound that formed the official residence or in the vicinity.

Kathli, as the smallest, most tender of the raw fruit was colloquially called, was carefully picked by the household help, brought home, peeled painstakingly after their palms had quite literally been greased, cut lengthwise into rectangles and then lovingly bhunoed just like pieces of tender goat meat chops would be. The treatment of both the meat and vegetarian dishes was quite the same: slow-cooking in yoghurt, with a substantial addition of onions and whole and powdered spices like badi elaichi, or black cardamom with its nutty aroma, cinnamon, cloves, et al. No tomatoes were used – no one would think of using these as the souring agent in a meat curry, after all. True to the Mughal style of cooking, yoghurt was the souring agent of choice and bhuna was the main method of cooking both vegetables and meats.

Jackfruit was also used in tahiri – the vegetarian equivalent of a meat pulao. But first, let us get the definitions right. There is no such thing as 'veg biryani' and a pulao *always* means a goat meat pulao. Belonging to a Kayasth family means that a little bit of food snobbery inevitably exists in your bloodstream, and even though I am quite democratic in my tastes, my blood rages just a little bit each time I find people – and restaurant menus – waxing eloquent about 'veg biryani' or 'veg pulao'.

Vegetables cooked with rice constitute a tahiri, not vegetable pulao or biryani. For instance, there is aloo ki tahiri – rice with potatoes. Here the aloo is cut lengthwise, added to the basic tempering of cumin seeds in ghee, sautéed to get a golden colour before long-grained, old rice is added and similarly sautéed, to coat each grain with fat and flavour. Then just enough water is added to cook the rice and the potato together till both are fully cooked but not mushy. Then there are matar ki tahiri, rice with green peas; gajar–gobhi ki tahiri, rice with carrots and cauliflower; even mangori ki tahiri, rice with dried lentil dumplings. It's as simple as that. Tahiri is a word you rarely come across today, certainly never on restaurant menus. But whatever they say about a rose, it is important to get the nomenclature correct! In our family tahiri was an everyday sort of lunch dish, the vegetables varying with the season. On special occasions, there was always a meat pulao. True to their medieval, Mughal-influenced roots, Kayasths have always prided themselves on the pulao on their tables. It is much subtler and purer than the everything-bunged-in biryani, though the latter too crept into Kayasth kitchens. But those are differences we shall deal with in a separate chapter.

Unlike matar ki tahiri – a mundane sort of dish – kathal ki tahiri was a rather more exotic preparation. It required selecting the right sort of tender, raw jackfruit and then cooking the tahiri in such a way that it resembled goat meat pulao. Jackfruit pieces were first bhunoed with whole spices and onions in ghee and yoghurt, and then cooked along with the rice till both the rice and vegetable were fully done and tender. This required a fair bit of expertise since the tahiri – like a pulao – needed to emerge as an unmashed concoction, each grain of rice standing separate, infused with flavour, and the vegetable remaining soft but firm in texture. The tahiri would be served garnished with browned onions just like a pulao and with a raita. It made for a great party dish – and continues as one in my home, despite seasonal vegetables falling out of favour with globalized palates.

Kofte could be made into a faux non-vegetarian dish, too. The vegetarian kofte that are now fairly common in north Indian cooking started out that way. Talk to an average diner in UP, Delhi, Bihar, Madhya Pradesh, even Rajasthan, and other regions about kofte and the mental picture that is conjured up is of the humble lauki ke kofte that is put out on lunch tables in many homes in summer. It is a rather old-fashioned dish – something that went out of style at least thirty years ago. Bottle gourd boiled, the water squeezed out, mixed with roasted gram flour, fried into rounds and put in a curry. No one would put it on a party menu these days, for sure; it is a homely dish. But, despite its extreme democratization, the genesis of kofte is quite interesting.

For one, despite the assumption in north India today that kofte must inevitably be vegetarian, they are, in fact, one of the earliest non-vegetarian dishes of the subcontinent. In Iran and Turkey, as also in Armenia, Egypt and other parts of the Arab world, the Persian-derived word *kofta* means minced meat spiced with parsley, mint and light seasoning, grilled on a wooden stick/skewer – almost like the Indian seekh kebab, which is also made of lamb mince (though chicken versions are available nowadays) though it is flavoured with stronger spices and more elongated in shape, besides being grilled differently. It is quite ironical, really, that in India we think only of vegetarian kofte.

Without doubt, the seekh kebab has its ancestor in the Persian kofta. So do all the many Indian kofte – both non-vegetarian and vegetarian versions – all of which are specialities of the Kayasth repertoire. Kachche keeme ke kofta – rounds of spiced goat meat mince and simmered in gravy – are legendary in Kayasth hospitality. Busy housewives would excel at these, briskly rolling out the perfect rounds on Sunday afternoons or when surprise guests came calling. But if the meat kofta is one of the big-ticket Kayasth dishes, so are the vegetarian versions that must have come up to placate the palate of the mostly vegetarian Kayasth women, who so excelled at making the meat kofte. And so the vegetarian kofte were born in the unique way in which Indian kitchens have blended together disparate influences to produce distinct subcontinental dishes, substituting ingredients, using more spices and so on. From those made out of bottle gourd to other less common varieties fashioned from raw jackfruit, raw banana, spinach and apricots, khoya (condensed milk), potatoes and more, kofte became omnipresent in the north Indian kitchen thanks perhaps to the Kayasths.

In my family, moong dal kofte was the big thing. The lentil was ground and then dried and sautéed in a little ghee in a wok with subtle spicing and enough ginger and garlic to be reduced to a sticky paste. It was then made into little rounds, which were fried and cooked in a gravy of onions, spices and yoghurt. When done well, moong dal kofte could indeed be passed off as meat kofte and were fairly addictive.

Like the vegetarian kofta, traditionally, the vegetarian kebab didn't exist either. All those who swear by their hara bhara and navrattan seekh kebabs hopefully know that what they are eating are primarily restaurant creations to take care of the 'veg veto'. In every group of diners, even those frequenting restaurants known primarily for their non-vegetarian food, there will invariably be some strict vegetarians. If the restaurant fails to cater to them – whatever be the cuisine it is offering and whether or not that cuisine has vegetarian dishes in its fold – it loses business. Vegetarian kebabs were essentially developed by north Indian restaurants to offer something more exotic than home-style food to vegetarian diners who accompanied the non-vegetarians wishing to sample tandoor-grilled meats and later the qormas and curries that gained popularity as restaurant food in India, post Partition.

I am not really a fan of either the vegetarian kofte or the vegetarian kebabs, an indistinct mishmash where you don't know what you are eating except for the spices. In fact, one of the most appalling wastes I have seen in restaurant kitchens in recent times have been by way of the guchchi kofta – where whole morels, worth their weight in gold, are pummelled to make somewhat of a 'royal' kofta, coated with *varq*, a thin gold sheet.

Recipes

Kele ki Machchli

This is a mock fish preparation invented by Mrs LC, it seems, for the benefit of LC when he turned vegetarian in later years. It was a summer favourite in our home, best had with arhar dal and chawal.

Serves 4

INGREDIENTS

The 'fillets'

- 6 raw bananas, sliced as 'fillets'
- 100g besan (gram flour)
- Salt to taste
- 1 tsp red chilli powder
- ½ tsp garam masala powder
- 1 tbsp chopped coriander
- 1 tsp carom seeds
- 1 tsp amchoor powder
- Oil to fry

The gravy

- 2 cups grated onion
- 1 tsp ginger paste
- 1 tsp garlic paste
- 1 tsp turmeric powder

1 tsp coriander powder
Salt to taste
½ tsp red chilli powder
½ cup fresh tomato purée
Water
2 tbsp kasoori methi (dried fenugreek leaves)

METHOD

Mix besan with all the dry masalas and add some water to it to make a thick paste.

Dip the banana pieces in this and deep-fry in a kadhai till golden and crisp. Keep aside.

Now, in a separate deep pan, sauté the grated onions till pink.

Add the ginger and garlic pastes, as well as the turmeric, red chilli powder and salt. Sauté.

Add the tomato purée and cook well till the oil floats on top and the masala is well done, about 10 minutes.

Add water to create the consistency of a thick gravy.

Just before serving, boil the gravy, add the 'fish' pieces to this and let it simmer for 2–3 minutes for the flavours to blend.

Finish by crushing kasoori methi with your palms and adding this to the dish for aroma.

Mangori–Matar ki Tahiri

This was usually a light summer lunch. A single dish meal, where rice, dal – by way of the mangori – and seasonal vegetables were combined together flavourfully.

Serves 4

INGREDIENTS

- 4 tbsp ghee
- 2 large onions, sliced
- Whole garam masala
  - 2 bay leaves
  - 4-5 cloves
  - 2 big black cardamom, crushed
  - 1 stick cinnamon
- 1kg long-grained Basmati rice, washed and soaked for 30 minutes
- 500g fresh green peas
- 250g sundried mangori, fried till reddish brown
- Salt to taste
- Water

METHOD

In a heavy-bottomed pan, heat ghee and add the sliced onions, fry till golden.

Now, add the whole spices and stir-fry for a minute till they release their aroma.

Drain the rice. Add to the spices and onion and stir-fry for a minute or two, till the ghee coats the grains.

Now add the fresh green peas, mangori and enough water to cook the rice with so that the grains remain separate.

Add salt and cover and cook till the rice is cooked but not mashed. The peas will cook along with the rice and the mangori will become tender.

Serve hot with papad, achar and raita.

Dal ke Kofte

These are simple, home-style kofte made to approximate the non-vegetarian lunch dish that most Kayasth women cooked but didn't eat. To pep these up, you could also place a sliver of almond in the centre of each kofta before frying.

Serves 4

INGREDIENTS

500g split and husk-less moong dal, soaked for 1 hour
100g or 1 cup of ghee
A big pinch of asafoetida
Oil for frying
1kg onions, grated
100g ginger paste
50g garlic paste
½ tsp turmeric powder
1 tsp red chilli powder
Salt to taste
500g fresh tomato purée
2 tsp garam masala
Water

METHOD

Drain the moong dal and grind to a paste without adding any water.

Now, in a kadhai, add the ghee, add the heeng and sauté the dal paste till it is fragrant and golden. You will need to constantly stir this to prevent the dal from sticking to the kadhai. Once the dal is cooked and fragrant, take the kadhai off the flame. Let the paste cool.

In a separate kadhai, pour the oil and add the grated onion. When this is golden brown, add the ginger and garlic pastes, and stir-fry for 10 minutes.

Add salt, turmeric and red chilli. Now add the tomato purée and keep stirring till the masala is well cooked and the oil floats on top, about 5–7 minutes.

Add about 4 tbsp of this masala to the cooling dal. Add 1 tsp of garam masala and shape into small rounds, or kofte.

Deep-fry the kofte till golden brown. Remove with a slotted spoon on some kitchen paper.

Now, heat the rest of the masala and add water to make a thin gravy. Bring to a boil. Gently drop the kofte into the gravy. Simmer for 5 minutes.

Sprinkle 1 tsp of garam masala on top and serve hot with parathas or rice.

6

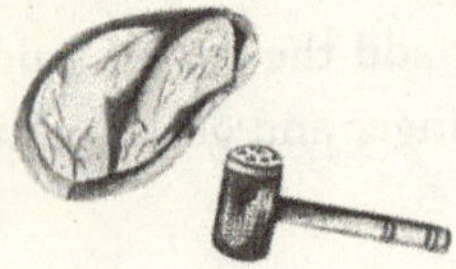

The Stronghold of Pasanda and Pulao

The Big-ticket Red Meat Dishes

Strangely enough, while growing up in Lucknow, I don't remember ever eating the fabled pasande. It was one of those exotic dishes that one had only heard about but never tasted or cooked. From time to time I would hear people reminisce about the flawless dish cooked by some family elder or the other (most often of by my father's aunt, Mrs KC) and I would mentally conjure up pictures about the cooking method, which seemed inordinately long and laborious. Mr and Mrs LC had by then settled with my chacha, post retirement from their bureaucratic Railway lives. My own parents, in whom the Mathur gene was somewhat more diluted, followed many other community customs but, alas, never the ritual of making pasande – by far the best-known and most heavy-duty of Kayasth main courses.

With the family home, Raghunath House in Moradabad, being sold off with the passing of my great-grandfather

Pradyumn Krishna, I never did have an ancestral home, the sense of roots, of visiting a place where my ancestors had lived during summer vacations. I have no memories of dal cooking in earthenware with bits of raw mango, or of pasande judiciously soaking up masala and ghee, the rogan or layer of fat rising to the top, not to be skimmed off by health-conscious diners but admired for its unique taste by pleasure-seekers, the shaukeen men and women of that generation, or of the Akhand Ramayana being read out aloud through entire days and nights, neighbours joining in so that the recitation of verses could carry on without a break, or of long mushairas where self-composed verses were read out.

Yet, although I haven't inhaled first-hand the aroma of that world, I did grow up on vivid accounts of other people's food (and culture) memories. This was part of the charm – and I say this in hindsight – of growing up in a Kayasth family, the other huge part consisting, of course, of daily access to a lavish table laid out with plenty of good and experimental food. I remember animated discussions on whether the langda was superior to the dussehri (no one talked about alphonsos at all, or ate them, till much later when the family became more globalized), or debates as to the merit of the Dilli bedmi versus the UP kachori. If, as a toddler, I had been regaled by Barima with the gajar ka halwa recipe narrated like a bedtime story, as an adolescent afternoon naps with her – when my grandparents spent several months with us at a stretch – were punctuated by snatches of bhajans and, well, the pasanda processes she tried to teach me.

The pasanda is a flat and prime cut of meat, traditionally carved out from the leg of the goat. The trick lies in the cut of the meat itself; the flat meat should be further hammered with a wooden mallet to make it thinner, so that it can be rolled and will cook evenly and easily. The cut is one that few butchers do today, or even know about. When my grandparents were around, families stuck to their own meat shops and personally went to buy the cuts they preferred. In Mughal and 'upper-class' kitchens it was regarded as a prime or choice cut; hence the name, with its obvious roots in the Urdu *pasand* or choice. As the name suggests, pasanda was a special-occasion, 'royal' dish, not an everyday curry for the table. It was a dish for entertaining. Much before I eventually tasted it, I had already tasted it in my mind thanks to my grandparents' vivid descriptions and, inevitably, the dish in my mind has always tasted finer.

Many of the fabulous pasanda cooks, the older Kayasth women with traditional recipes that had been handed down, are no longer around. One such was Mrs KC, my grandfather's sister-in-law. Legendary for her 'good hands', referred to as such both for the deliciousness they concocted and the ease and speed with which they did so. She was the great meat cook of the family. The kaliya she cooked was held up as the shining beacon of Kayasth cooking, as was the pasanda. The LCs strongly subscribed to the 'good hands' theory, and I am a believer in it myself because of the family's history of cooking such delicacies as badam pasanda. It is a concept often dismissed by modern chefs. To run a restaurant, standardization and precision are two pillars of cooking. But cooking is not entirely a science; it is an art form too – an individual's expression of herself or himself. That is why there are talented, instinctive cooks, masters of taste, the flavour of whose cooking can never be replicated by anyone else even if the recipe is followed perfectly.

The classic Mathur Kayasth recipe for badam pasande from old Delhi involves lots of blanched and peeled almonds. Slivers of these would be cut and stuffed inside each piece of meat, which would be rolled up and tied with a thread. To cook this delicacy even in smaller batches was no mean task; for a large wedding or party it was obviously a mammoth undertaking. The stuffed pasande would be marinated in yoghurt, spices and kachri powder made from a local berry, the tenderizing agent of choice in Kayasth kitchens. These pieces of meat would then be left to cook in a simmering onion gravy, and the rest of the almonds added to the gravy for texture.

I have always found the choice of the tenderizer quite interesting. Mughal-inspired cooking traditionally uses raw papaya as an ingredient to soften meat. Papain, the protease in papaya skin, is the softening agent. Papaya is a common enough ingredient in the subcontinent; in fact, India is the largest grower of papaya today. Yet, the Hindu Kayasth kitchen preferred to use dried kachri, a cucumber-like sour fruit that grows wild in jowar fields primarily in Rajasthan and western UP, for this purpose. Village kids in these regions are known to nibble on the fruit despite its sharp and pungent flavour.

How did this rustic element find its way into the cooking of the Kayasths? We can only speculate. As an indigenous, wild ingredient from the region where the community possibly originated, this must have been a natural preference. Papaya, by contrast, found its way from South America to India via south-east Asia. One of the fallouts of the Columbian Exchange – the exchange of plants, technology, culture and humans between America, Europe and their colonies in Asia and Africa after Christopher Columbus discovered America in the fifteenth century – was that Spanish colonists carried the seeds of the papaya plant to the Philippines in 1550. From here it spread to India, probably around the time when the first Kayasths were finding favour within the existing political order of the day and imbibing snippets of courtly culture. The imported ingredient, however, may not have been in common use then. While the Mughal royal cooks, with access to the finest ingredients, may have experimented with papaya in their cuisine, it is possible that the Kayasths stuck to homely cooking styles and native ingredients. Other communities did the same. Even in the hardy Rajput cooking, for instance, papaya never replaced kachri as a tenderizer for meats.

Mrs KC's badam pasande was an intricate work of art.

This traditional dish is hardly available now, even within Kayasth homes. What I have come across at special lunches and weddings and festive occasions is the shorter version – where the pasande are not rolled up and tied. Instead, the flat pieces of meat are left to cook in gravy with a whole lot of almonds added into it. Even this is a spectacular dish. My father makes it to perfection and it has become the trademark dish of our family.

From shami kebab to kaliya, keema mirch and more, sometimes the only difference between the non-vegetarian, mutton-centric repertoire of Kayasth homes and the home-style Muslim cuisine from Delhi/UP is only a change of name. Ishtoo, the now somewhat elusive but well-known old Delhi Muslim dish (its name a corruption of the word 'stew'), is in fact the same as the old Delhi Kayasth khade masale ka bhuna gosht. Both come from Shahjahanabad, where the communities co-existed for centuries in close proximity. Both are essentially dishes where the mutton is layered with a host of onions and khada masala, or whole spices (including black pepper, distinctive to old Delhi), and left to, literally, stew in its own juices till deliciously tender, with the masala getting bhunoed in the process of slow-cooking and not separately. The badam pasanda, though, is fairly distinctive. UP and even Pakistani (Punjab) homes cook the pasande as a quick snack – marinating the flat pieces in yoghurt and cream, ginger, garlic and spices, and pan-grilling them. It is similar to the *paarchey* that you may come across in restaurant kitchens – though these days, the term pasanda is so abused that restaurants use it for anything from chicken escalope to prawns!

Traditionally, pasanda was made from beef or lamb/goat meat and the Kayasth version is distinctive in being a heavy-duty, curried main course. It is also perhaps one of the few recipes in the Kayasth repertoire to use almonds, or any nuts, and dried fruit. Unlike the Mughal kitchens influenced by Persian traditions, where recipes turned increasingly elaborate and rich as the empire became established and emperors became avid patrons of the arts, including culinary art, Kayasth non-vegetarian food remained firmly home-style. The table was lavish but the recipes made use of easily accessed ingredients: onions, yoghurt, seasonal vegetables and fruits. For instance, it was common to find fried arvi in a mutton curry in summer and radish and carrots in the sublime, slow-cooked shabdeg in winter; all these were essentially home-style curries and stews.

This characteristic of Kayasth cooking – its home-style-nature and its use of easy-to-find ingredients – extends to other aspects, such as the aroma of the food. Like other Mughal-influenced food, which is distinguished by its use of aromatic spices, Kayasth khana too typically stresses on *khushbu* – the aroma or appetizing smell of the food. In fact, dining in Indian homes has traditionally been a multi-sensory experience, despite the image of curry as a sloppily served-up mishmash, at least in the minds of people only exposed to restaurant Indian food, not to mention the typical curry houses of the West. Dishes and combinations of dishes served together as part of a single meal have always juxtaposed flavours and textures, and the aroma of food has been layered, nuances and just as important as the food's visual or palate appeal.

In Kayasth cooking, the intrinsic smell or 'meatiness' of a non-vegetarian dish is camouflaged by the use of spice powders sprinkled over the dish post cooking. But instead of fancy aromatics, the spices used are simple, easily accessible ones like chhoti elaichi (green cardamom) powder, javitri (mace) and jaiphal (nutmeg), and sometimes kebabchini (allspice), now rarely available in stores. At times a few drops of kewra, or screw pine, essence can be judiciously added to the curry. But an extensive use of sweet essence – rose water, screwpine and the *meetha itar* of Mughal cooking – is conspicuous by its absence. Nor is expensive saffron added to any dish to enhance its colour and flavour, unlike in other Mughal-influenced cooking, where a few strands are added to the rice or a dessert. But then, home-style cooking, whether Hindu or Muslim, has not really used these ingredients, many of which are now common in commercial cooking.

As I've mentioned earlier, Barima was not a particularly keen cook. Brought up as a pampered almost-royal, she was efficient in running the household with the help of a large contingent of staff, would entertain and socialize lavishly but not venture into the kitchen on a daily basis. However, there were particular dishes whose cooking she would never delegate to anyone else. The shami kebab was one these.

She made the kebabs to perfection – tender, bursting with the flavour of mint leaves, with just the right bite of spicing and green chillies.

At home, we still follow my grandmother's recipe. The trick to a good shami kebab is not just in choosing meat with enough fat to keep it juicy and moist but also in the proportion of chana dal cooked with the mince to hold it all together. The proportion of the chana dal, split Bengal gram, to the keema needs to be a strict 200 grams to a kilo of minced meat. A higher proportion of the dal would dry out the kebab, while a lower proportion would lead to the kebab not holding shape during frying. Enough green cardamom powder has to be added to the mince to mask the meatiness. The kebabs need to be carefully stuffed with green chillies, mint and/or finely diced raw onion to give a burst of freshness and texture when you bite into one. Finally, they are pan-fried in their own fat, patiently, till each one is evenly brown on the outside and juicy and moist inside. In Kayasth homes, the technique used has always been a shallow fry done on a tawa, using minimal oil or ghee; the natural fat of the meat would be enough to brown the kebab. (The 'commercialized' shami kebab that you sometimes find at catered dos and even at celebrated eateries, where chunky meat patties are crumbed and fried, would undoubtedly have filled Barima with horror. After all, they are not 'shami kebab'!) I don't know whether it is nostalgia, fact or perception. But however faithfully we follow Barima's recipe, the distinctive taste of her cooking has been impossible to replicate.

Mrs KC, the pasanda expert, was equally known for her kaliya. Kaliya, a basic meat curry, cooked by the bhuna method, was an everyday sort of dish. Yet, the Kayasth kaliya, browned properly and with some oil floating on top, is quite a revered dish. I have come across quite a few recipients of Kayasth hospitality who talk about this dish with great nostalgia. Every home tweaked the spices according to their own family recipe. But mostly these were just the simple turmeric, chilli and coriander powder of home cooking, used judiciously, with an aromatic like cardamom powder added at the end. The trick to a good kaliya was just in the bhunoing, the slow roasting of the meat and onions to concentrate the flavour. It required patience – and 'good hands'.

Mrs LC hardly ever made the humble kaliya, but she was certainly the yakhni pulao champion, the expert maker of this king of the Kayasth culinary repertoire – goat meat pulao cooked in stock. 'Yakhni' refers to meat stock, not the curd-based sauce for meat that many people who associate the term only with Kashmiri cooking take it for. Barima taught the dish to her daughters-in-law, who cook it with their own individual expressions (except my mother, because in our home it is my father who is in charge of cooking all things non-vegetarian), but her yakhni pulao was the original and a classic, each grain of rice getting its burst of flavour from the yakhni in which it had been cooked. When she supervised its cooking, it seemed to be a simple enough dish, but, struggling to replicate it in hotel kitchens as part of the Kayasth food promotions that I curate and cook for, I have realized how deceptive that simplicity is.

Unlike at home, where all the family cooks – my dad, mum, aunts – are fairly dexterous and can control all the processes involved in cooking the yakhni pulao, in restaurant kitchens we invariably make the stock and then hand it over to commercially trained chefs. They are the ones who then cook the rice in it, steaming it in huge *lagans*, heavy copper pots with a wide mouth and a curved base sealed with dough in the process called dum. But most restaurants do not really understand, or rather follow, the dum or any slow-cooking. It is not commercially viable, since turnaround demands are high and time is at a premium. Most restaurant chefs lead to à la minute cooking, figuring out shortcuts even for Indian dishes that call for slow-cooking for the proper assimilation of flavours. I have seen curries being cooked in frying pans for room-service orders, ketchup being added to the onion gravy, and meat being boiled and dunked in the masala at the last minute to fill up the buffet when food is running short late in the night. Inevitably, under these circumstances, yakhni pulao never turns out right because the junior chefs, who are in charge of such jobs as cooking rice, boil the Basmati rice separately, layer the meat with it, and finally faux-dum this (for a couple of minutes) to dutifully serve up the pulao. This, of course, is not pulao at all.

Mrs LC was snobbish about the pulao. The first thing you learned was to keep the pressure cooker away. In fact, no rice in our house was ever cooked in a pressure cooker. Not even a humble aloo ki tahiri. To have each grain of rice separate and standing firm was the hallmark of any superior rice dish – except if you were making a khichdi, where the mashed texture was intrinsic to the blending of the dal and rice flavours. (But there were also different types of khichdi and one using arhar dal, for instance, could not be soupy at all but required the grains of the dal and rice to remain separate.) In any case, if the rice stuck, the pulao was a failure. Each grain of rice also had to be coated with enough flavour from both the ghee in which it was first roasted and then the stock in which it was boiled, for the preparation to be perfect.

The deep stainless steel pots with heavy bases, called *bhagonas*, in which Barima cooked were perfect for this. I remember a time, very early on, when the household used heavy brassware for dishes that would take longer to cook. But when kalai-wallas, who would roam the streets and 'tin' these utensils, that is, coat the cooking surface with a powder to prevent the copper in the alloy from reacting with acids during the cooking process and turning poisonous, became non-existent in Lucknow, the household gradually shifted entirely to cooking in steel.

The process of making yakhni for the pulao would start with the generous addition of ghee to the pot, followed by a host of whole spices, including badi elaichi, or black cardamom. The meat would then be added along with some whole onions, garlic and ginger. The meat cuts would have been carefully selected; my grandmother favoured the quick-to-cook chops and some 'gol boti', boneless pieces from the thigh, apart from pieces of the raan, thigh bones, and all that had maximum flavour. When the stock bubbled and boiled and the meat was about 40 per cent cooked, this would be taken out carefully, the stock strained and preserved. Then would come the bhunoing of the meat pieces: the pieces would be carefully browned in another pot with grated onions, more garam masala, ginger, garlic and yoghurt.

'Now, you have to be very careful to judge that the meat is 70 per cent done at this stage,' Barima would instruct. For someone who did not eat meat, it is a wonder how she judged so precisely the extent to which the meat had cooked, without either tasting or even touching it to check its texture. Once the meat had been adequately bhunoed, rice would be added, as well as just enough stock to cook both the rice and the meat together in a warm and wonderful mass that would finally result in our comforting lunch dish. Yakhni pulao, when it emerged steaming hot from the kitchen, would announce its arrival with its aroma; the meat would fall off the bone perfectly when one touched a spoon to it, but its real charm lay in the taste of the rice, the original Basmati flavour coated with stock, spices and ghee. It was the perfect understated gourmet dish.

In another version of the yakhni pulao the flavour of saunf, or fennel seeds, is a highlight. One evening, I watched

Anil Chandra, Chef Manu Chandra's father and an excellent home cook, like my own father and many Kayasth men of that generation, as he went about the painstaking process of making stock, sautéing the meat, tempering the rice itself and finally cooking both together in stock on dum. The recipe he used was more or less similar to Mrs LC's. But while Mrs LC did not emphasize the use of fennel seeds in the garam masala that is boiled along with the meat to make the stock, for Mr Chandra saunf is a mandatory ingredient. He attributes this to the Kashmiri influence, which I write about in more detail in the next chapter.

In comparison to yakhni pulao, the biryani was the more robust wannabe on the table. Mrs LC spared no thought to it at all. In her house, it was only made on days when leftover meat curry needed to be reused. The curry would be reduced and layered with pre-cooked rice, enterprising cooks would add some browned onions and fried nuts to the concoction, sprinkle some chopped mint leaves along with some milk to moisten it all up, and drop in a trace of kewra essence. But this was really a spiced-up pretender to the gourmet throne. No one waxed poetic about it.

In the world outside my family, things were wildly different. Biryani was the star. Few really understood – or sometimes even knew of – the pulao. Since I began writing on food, I have noticed that much is made of biryani by food 'experts' as well. The immense, pan-India popularity of the dish means that it is a great topic for columns and television shows, for all manner of research and food trails.

We too bought our share of biryani (and kali mirch chicken and seekh kebab) from the assorted shops near the K.D. Singh Babu Stadium in Lucknow on special occasions, partaking of the great Avadhi heritage with gusto. Avadhi biryani has now been branded as 'pakki biryani', because the meat and rice are fully cooked before they are layered and cooked in dum. It has gained much renown, thanks in part to accomplished Muslim chefs of five-star hotels who brought their cooking methods, nomenclature and stories into the five-star fold, creating a whole genre of food with heritage underpinnings that can also be easily marketed. However, I am not particularly a fan of Avadhi biryani.

If biryani is as much about the spice as about the rice and meat, I would any day prefer its Hyderabadi kachchi version, where raw, marinated meat is layered with rice and cooked on dum. It has far more flavour and uses more interesting spices than its Avadhi cousin. The best biryanis to my mind are the northern Kerala Moplah biryani from the fishermen's community and the chemeen biryani of the Syrian Christians, both of which are tremendously flavourful. Should one wish for something subtler and more sophisticated, there is nothing to beat a well-cooked yakhni pulao – a dish requiring superior cooking skills, in my opinion, to what any biryani does.

There are various theories about the pulao and the biryani. The pulao, it is commonly believed, has a Persian pedigree, referring to a rice dish cooked in stock, served with or without meat on top. As such it is a dry dish; if meat is served with it, it is a dry meat, placed on top of the rice. This is true for almost all variants of the dish found throughout Turkey, Afghanistan, the Baltic and Arab regions. Pulao, in fact, is quite an ancient dish, as the Greek *pilafi* testifies. References to it have been made in Macedonian literature of the time of Alexander's conquests. It was a common dish of the Ottoman state and must have entered India before the Mughal period, perhaps during the Turkish–Afghan period of our medieval history. We don't quite know when it was incorporated into the Kayasth repertoire but it must have been fairly early on, because the yakhni pulao, while including more whole spices than the simpler pilafi or pulows of elsewhere, is still quite a pristine dish that uses subtler spices. The biryani, on the other hand, is a very different dish, even if it is a relative of the pulao. Some food historians trace the word to *birinj*, meaning rice in Persian; others to *biryan*, meaning frying the rice in oil. Still others distinguish the biryani as a dish that layers meat and rice – a sandwich of sorts. My grandparents believed the layering was just a trick, hardly the essence of the dish. A biryani in its basic form was held to be simply a more heavily spiced pulao – a dish where we cooked the rice and the meat separately and then bunged them together. It was certainly less sophisticated than the carefully controlled pulao.

What I believe is that the pulao, the original royal dish, got Indianized as it travelled through the sub-continent, incorporating more and more spices as post-Mughal cooks experimented with it, adding local ingredients to the basic dish and tweaking the cooking process. Some even replaced the meat with potatoes when the former got too expensive. That's the story behind the Calcutta biryani, version of the Avadhi biryani. It is believed that the cooks of the exiled Nawab Wajid Ali Shah substituted potatoes for half the meat in the dish. Certainly, the biryani became democratized with its rising popularity among 'commoners'.

The theory that the biryani is just a spiced-up pulao is supported by the fact that the cooking processes of the yakhni pulao, as made in my home, and the Hyderabadi biryani are much the same despite the different flavour profiles. Both the pulao and the Hyderabadi kachchi biryani use raw meat and rice, cooked together in a sealed pot. And that, I feel, is the basic common feature that puts them in the same category. The differences in spices and treatment of the meat are merely evolutionary; the Hyderabadi preparation inevitably shows Deccani influence in terms of the spices it incorporates, uses a more sophisticated marinade of raw papaya and, being a chronologically later dish, shows signs of improvisation by Nizami cooks to do away with the multiple processes involved in making the pulao. The layering of rice and meat was probably a way to have an even distribution of meat and rice given the girth of the vessels they were cooked in; it may have been simply an outcome of functionality.

If the Avadhi biryani, which is a pakki biryani and spiced as subtly as a pulao, and the Hyderabadi biryani, which is a kachchi biryani, cooked quite like a yakhni pulao but with more robust spices, are the 'royal' rice dishes, invented for courts and the 'upper' classes, there are other rice-with-spice-and-meat dishes with more plebeian origins throughout the subcontinent. Trading communities along India's coast interacted with the Arab world and the exchange of ingredients and ideas resulted in other biryanis such as the Sindhi, Moplah and Suriani. These are a different genre, I believe, with a different evolution. They are essentially dishes with rice and spices available along the Spice Route, bits of local seafood or meat – the same genre as, say, the nasi goreng of Indonesia or even the paella of Spain. Essentially, these are dishes of the common people along the coast, prepared using the ingredients best representing their regions. The yakhni pulao or the Hyderabadi kachchi biryani, on the other hand, are courtly creations that have seeped into our popular culinary culture top down. As for the 'biryani' cooked in our home, it was, as it always claimed to be, a shortcut – adopted by cooks and housewives alike.

That biryani is a dish inferior to pulao, which requires much more dexterity in its preparation; that it is a plebeian dish while pulao is more courtly; and that Hyderabadi kachchi biryani and all Kayasth pulaos are related in some way are all my threories. I don't know what the LCs would have made of them.

Recipes

Yakhni Pulao

Some family recipes also use a fistful of saunf, or fennel seeds, in the whole garam masala used to flavour the yakhni (stock).

INGREDIENTS

- 50–100g ghee
- 150g onions, chopped
- 50g garlic, chopped
- 25g ginger, chopped
- Salt to taste
- 500g goat meat, curry cut
- 4 glasses of water
- 500g rice
- 50g yoghurt
- Whole garam masala
  - 4 black cardamoms
  - 10 cloves
  - 15–20 black peppercorns
  - 10 green cardamoms
  - 2 bay leaves
- 3 tbsp coriander powder
- Red chilli powder to taste
- 1 tbsp garam masala powder

1 tsp green cardamom powder
1 cup browned onions for garnish

METHOD

Add half of the ghee to a heavy-bottomed deep pan or kadhai. Add half the chopped onions, ginger and garlic in it. Add salt.

Now add the meat with about 4 glasses of water. Put the whole garam masala into the pot. Cover and cook till meat is partially (50 per cent) cooked, about 20–25 minutes. Remove the meat, strain and reserve the stock (yakhni).

In a separate pan or kadhai, add the remaining ghee and the rest of the cut onion, garlic and ginger. Sauté they turn golden brown, add the boiled meat. Add coriander and red chilli powders and bhuno (sauté) for about 15 minutes.

Add the yoghurt and sauté for another 10 minutes till the meat is 80–85 per cent cooked.

Sprinkle the cardamom and garam masala powders for aroma.

Now, add washed Basmati rice and the reserved yakhni to the meat. Cover and let it cook on a low flame for about 15 minutes, till the rice is fully cooked.

Serve the pulao with a layer of browned onion on top.

Badam Pasande

Pasanda is a flat, boneless cut of meat that only a few butchers know how to carve. The meat is taken off the shanks and beaten to flatten it and tenderized to cook. Kachri powder is a natural tenderizer and also imparts sourness to the gravy.

Ingredients

1kg goat meat pasande
250g yoghurt
Salt to taste
50g garlic paste
100g kachri powder
150g almonds, soaked and peeled
50–100g refined oil (oil for frying onions is seperate)
100g onions
50g ginger paste
Red chilli powder to taste
250g tomatoes, freshly puréed
2 cups of water
2 tbsp garam masala powder
2–3 drops kewra essence

Method

Clean and wash the meat pieces, drain. Mix well 100g of beaten yoghurt, half of the garlic paste, salt and kachri powder, and marinate the pasande in this. Keep aside for about 45 minutes.

Make a paste of half the almonds and keep aside.

Fry the finely chopped onions till brown. Now crush them with your hands or in a blender and keep aside.

In a deep pan, add oil and sauté the ginger and almond pastes and the rest of the garlic paste till golden brown and aromatic, about 2–3 minutes. Add salt and red chilli powder.

Now add the fresh tomato purée and stir well for about 2–3 minutes till the oil separates and floats on top.

Add the remaining yoghurt and cook for a few minutes.

Then add the meat pieces with all the marinade. Add about

2 cups of water and the rest of the whole, peeled almonds. Let all this cook on a low flame for about 15–20 minutes. Now add the crushed, browned onions. You will see the gravy becoming richer and instantly getting more body. Let it simmer for 10–15 minutes for the flavours to blend and the pasande to be fully cooked. They should be tender enough to split with a spoon.

Finally, add the garam masala powder and the the kewra essence.

Enjoy the pasande with hot white rice or poori.

Shami Kebabs

The onion–mint–chillies stuffing in these kebabs added not just another burst of unexpected flavour and texture but also made them Mrs LC's specials. The trick is to have enough filling in the centre.

INGREDIENTS

- 500g keema
- 50–100g refined oil
- 2 large onions, finely chopped
- 10g garlic, chopped
- 10g ginger, chopped
- 125g chana dal
- Salt to taste
- Whole garam masala
  - 4 black cardamoms
  - 10 cloves

15–20 black peppercorns
10 green cardamom

2 bay leaves
1 glass of water
1 tsp green cardamom powder
1 tsp garam masala powder
1 cup fresh mint leaves, finely chopped
2 tbsp green chillies, finely chopped

METHOD

Clean and wash the mince. Drain.

In a pot, heat 1 tbsp of oil, and sauté one chopped onion, garlic and ginger till light brown.

Now, add the mince and the chana dal. Wrap all the whole garam masalas in a muslin cloth and tie the end to make a potli. Add salt and drop the muslin potli with the whole spices in as well. Add about one glass of water, or just enough to let the mince and dal cook till the keema is well done and the water totally evaporates.

Remove from the fire and let it cool.

Grind all the ingredients in a blender to make a fine paste. Add the green cardamom and garam masala powders for aroma and mix well.

Make a separate mix of the remaining chopped onion, and the mint leaves and green chillies.

Make small rounds of the ground mince, fill each with a little of the onion–mint leaves–green chillies mixture. Flatten into patties.

Pan-fry with very little oil or no oil (the keema should have enough fat of its own).

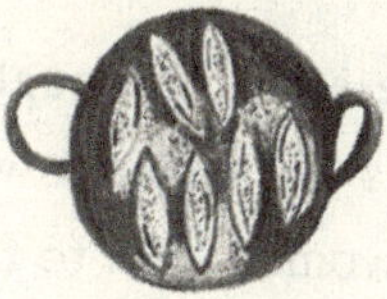

7

Unravelling Bharwan Karela

No Simple Veggies Here

When Barima was growing up in Gwalior, her father, Abbaji, was attached to the Scindia court and there were quite a few Kayasth families around for them to socialize with. But there was also plenty of other cross-cultural intermingling with families from across the country whose ancestors had sought employment with the Maratha courts. However, even in this relatively non-provincial set-up, interactions with Muslim families were minimal. My grandmother, despite possessing a prodigious talent for making friends and putting others at ease, did not have a single Muslim friend. According to her, any time they had a visitor from the 'other community' visiting, tea would be offered in separate crockery kept aside for such occasions. It was all terribly segregated in spite of the shared heritage of shami kebabs.

If there was the great chasm between Hindus and Muslims that centuries of working together in courts and sharing of cultural nuances had not bridged, there was an equally great divide between the sexes. Barima's early world was the world of the purdah as upper-class women took to the veil, as much to establish their social pedigree as to cover themselves from the prying male gaze. Everything from the women's quarters and classrooms to their tongas and cars were curtained. No ordinary man could peer inside, and no inner lives, perhaps, seep outside. When Barima and her sister went shopping, fawning shop owners would have their entire establishments emptied so that the semi-royal ladies could shop for clothing material or lace or jewellery or crockery in complete privacy. This social seclusion was a product of the great cultural mix of Hindustan – not solely Islamic, but something that had become part of the larger elite culture quite in the manner that music and food had. This was true, too, of the practice of eating leaves from the tamarind tree growing over the grave of Mian Tansen, the legendary singer of Akbar's court, who was from Gwalior and whose legacy lives on in the city in the hearts of both those Hindus and Muslims whose true allegiance is only to the Malhar.

In this world of segregation-yet-homogenization, Barima's greatest friend was Shanti Kaul, a lady of Kashmiri Pandit origin whose forefathers had left the Valley, another ancient melting pot of cultures, to settle in the plains of central India, serving Shivaji's *peshwa*s, or knight-kings, in the Deccan. Swaroop Rani and Shantiji shared their lives, their food and their histories. They were two individuals, not merely representatives of their larger communities. One consequence of this closeness was a dish that is a favourite in the family, even two generations down: methi chaaman. It is not a Kayasth dish but is nevertheless firmly a part of our family repertoire – loved, cherished and cooked regularly. Many special dinners and lunches prepared by Barima that I remember featured methi chaaman as its star vegetarian attraction. Fifty-odd years after it was taught to her by Shantiji, my grandmother did not abandon it – lovingly adding volumes of oil to the dried fenugreek leaves to roast them and take out the bitterness, making the chaaman (cottage cheese) at home, and using the leftover sour whey as a base for the thin curry. Like much of other home-style cooking throughout India, most Kayasth kitchens didn't experiment with cottage cheese till after Partition, when refugees from western Punjab (now in Pakistan) brought their tandoor and paneer into the mainstream pan-Indian consciousness. In my family, however, this ingredient had already sneaked its way into our hearts with such recipes earlier.

There seem to be other Kashmiri influences even in the larger food tradition of the Kayasth community. This was first pointed out to me by Anil Chandra while discussing the use of saunf in his excellent yakhni pulao. 'Many Kashmiri Pandits came down to UP to take up legal work at the Allahabad High Court,' he explained. We, of course, know of the Nehru family's legacy. But there were many more. Fennel, one of the ingredients that defines the cooking of

Kashmiri Pandits, became part of the Kayasth repertoire as a result of yet another intertwining of different cultural strands.

There may be more than a grain of truth to this observation. Dry saunf (powdered fennel seeds) is used in much of UP Kayasth cooking, including some speciality vegetarian dishes. Saunf powder is an integral part of the quintessential sookha masala (which also contains amchoor powder) used to stuff vegetables like ladies' finger, egg plant and bitter gourd. This spice mix, used in Kayasth cooking to transform many a summer vegetable from the mundane to the exalted, has a flavour profile fairly close to saunth (dry ginger powder) and saunf, common in Kashmiri cooking.

Despite this early experimentation with foods of other communities and regions, Barima was not an adventurous, or even an enthusiastic, diner by any means. Of the couple, it was always Papa who relished variety and novelty. It was for LC that in my house there would always be the piping-hot dish 'tapakti hui patta gobhi', cabbage freshly sautéed to remain al dente and served in a slight soup of its juices, on dreary winter afternoons when the sun refused to come out. It was for him that my mother would make besan laddoo with artificial sweeteners and my aunt bake eggless cakes (because, despite the onset of diabetes later in life, LC would not eschew *meetha*, sweet). And it was for him that my grandmother sometimes accompanied all of us to South Indian or Indian-Chinese restaurants though she ate neither cuisines and thought of restaurant cooking in general as unclean.

Just a few weeks before he died, as I accompanied him for a medical check-up, my grandfather spotted a McDonald's sign and wanted to stop for a burger. With confidence, I pacified him with the promise of 'next time'. There was no next time. The burger remained uneaten. A month after his death, as I served up a private meal of McD's to some kids in a private recreation of the shraadh my parents were doing elsewhere, I wished fervently that I had stopped that day for a McVeggie-with-cheese. With that time long lost, Papa's wish unfulfilled, the ritualistic feeding of the poor remained a lame, empty gesture of propitiation.

Barima, though infinitely choosy about the vegetables she ate, nevertheless had some favourites which were always safe options to include in her meal. Apart from pakori ki subzi, takey paise was by far her favourite main course, the dish for all occasions – when friends and relatives came calling or for Sunday lunch when the non-vegetarians binged on their kaliya, kofte and pulao.

As with so many vegetarian dishes served at the Kayasth table, this one too shares features in common with cuisines of other regions. Takey paise, termed as such across all Kayasth sub-castes, is actually a variation of the Marwari gatte ki sabzi. Chickpea flour or besan is kneaded into a supple dough, with the addition of enough oil, curd and grated onions (unlike the Marwari dish the Kayasth version uses onions) along with their water. This is rolled lengthwise into little cylinders; small rounds resembling coins (aka *takey* and *paise*, the small change) are then cut and fried till golden. These are delicious fritters in themselves that can be addictively snacked on. But the right way to finish the subzi curry is to let these rounds soak in a masala of onion and yoghurt. Although that is the Mathur version. Each sub-community makes takey paise slightly differently. I have seen Saxena homes do a dry version sans onions but with a lot of seasoning. The main difference between the recipes of the Marwari gatte and the Kayasth version seems to be that the fritters in the latter are fried instead of being steamed version and more heavily seasoned. Also, unlike in the Jodhpuri version, yoghurt is not the predominant flavour either in the small besan coins or the curry/masala.

We don't really know the story behind takey paise. Who gave it this name? How did a dish from the desert become so much a part of the Kayasth kitchen kinetics? Judging from its pervasive presence throughout the community's cooking and from the name itself, one can only conjecture that it is a fairly old dish of the community, improvised from some medieval recipe. It could perhaps be seen as one of those dishes that show up the pedigree of the Kayasths as the link community in Mughal India – between the Muslim courtiers and the Hindu courtiers, who were primarily Rajputs and Marwari moneylenders from Rajasthan. But this is merely conjecture too.

Potato was the single-most important vegetable in our kitchen, eaten whatever the season or time of the day, and with Barima, you could never go wrong with a couple of basics involving potatoes. Poori–aloo was the ultimate comfort dish in her book. My grandmother was happy to have aloo sautéed with her greens – methi in winter; sem, or broad beans, in summer – but what she liked best was to have them on their own in a mild curry.

The Dilli-style potato gravy eaten with bedmi is slightly different from the subzi you get with kachori or bedmi in UP. The former incorporates a chutney of soaked methi seeds as the primary flavouring agent for the curry. The methi seeds give it a tangy flavour as well as a lingering aftertaste, with just that tinge of bitterness to keep things interesting and astringent. If you have ever had a breakfast of bedai–aloo in Agra or kachori in Kanpur, you'll know that the UP potato curry differs from the one of Dilli. The UP curries go easy on fenugreek. Instead, they use more black pepper, and sometimes fresh green chillies, to spice up the dish. What we made at home was the same style of dish but with fresher, easier-to-find ingredients that added the required dash of tartness and punch to the gravy.

Tamatar aloo is the quintessential Mathur homely dish, with a burst of flavour obtained from tomatoes and fresh ginger. No onion or garlic is added. Instead, potatoes are boiled and roughly crumbled into a tempering of asafoetida and cumin seeds, with a touch of turmeric and salt. Once this basic spice mix coats the potatoes, smashed with the back of the spoon while cooking, roughly chopped tomatoes and ginger juliennes along with finely sliced green chillies and freshly chopped coriander leaves are added to the mishmash. This is then stirred a few times and water is added to the curry. It is then left to simmer and come to a boil, by which time the flavours would have blended in. Eaten with hot, puffed-up pooris, this is as delicious a meal as any fancier one.

Then there was the bhune hue aloo with parathas that we served Barima. This dry preparation, spiced with a simple mix of heeng, zeera, amchoor powder, once again gets its flavour from the process of slow-roasting in oil, the trademark Kayasth cooking process. Sometimes, potatoes cooked like this and patiently bhunoed for the good part of an hour in the kadhai would also be dubbed 'safari aloo' (from the word *safar*), because this was the usual preparation to pack (along with parathas and pickle) when you travelled to another town – the standard train meal most Kayasth families took along with them for sustenance and carb comfort.

In summer or when it rained and no fresh vegetables were available in the kitchen, potatoes could also be paired with mangoris in a curry. I remember one winter afternoon when my grandmother sat on the terrace, the mild sun casting a glow on her face, and showed me how to make the perfect mangori. She took little bits of ground moong dal in pinches between her thumb and ring finger and dropped the little pearls on clean newspaper sheets, in neat rows. The mangori had to be tiny and of even size if they were to win the approval of the stern perfection-seeking matriarchs from whom Barima had learned this art. The sun-dried mangori would be collected and stored away in air-tight jars for use during those seasons when vegetables were not easy to come by. Needless to say, no one after Barima bothered to perfect the art of making mangori from scratch; there is plenty of it available in kirana stores, made in ramshackle workshops by migrant women who come to the big cities from their villages and make industrial quantities of mangori and papad for daily wages.

The mangori is common to several communities in north India, primarily the Marwari community in Rajasthan – here we have another example of the culinary link between the cuisines of the Hindu powerati of the Mughal/Maratha eras, and the emerging Kayasth community. But, another lentil preparation, the mota papad, is a uniquely Mathur Kayasth innovation. Sheets of thick urad dal papad, flavoured with black pepper, are sun-dried and then cut in small dices and stored away. To prepare this lunch delicacy, all you need to do is fry the tiny bits of papad till they are golden and curry them with potatoes.

Lentil in the form of sun-dried, fermented dumplings is a uniquely north Indian tradition, particularly in Punjab, UP, Rajasthan and Gujarat. It is possibly a continuation of the tradition of eating papad as an accompaniment and a snack and finale to Indian cuisines throughout the subcontinent. The thin, flat bread-like but sun-dried papad is commonly made from spiced urad dal paste or other lentils, as are the dumplings, variously called vadi, badi, badiyan, or mangore. The seasoning changes with the type of dal that is used. The heavier urad dal badiyan from Amritsar, for instance, have a potent spice mix compared to the light mangori seasoned with just asafoetida and made from moong dal. In the Kayasth and more specifically the Mathur kitchen, the mota papad dish is made with small cubes cut from thick moong dal papads, sun-dried, fermented and seasoned with black pepper. Like mangori, the cubes are fried till they start giving off an aroma typical of roasted dal and turn reddish in colour. They are then curried and left in the liquid to soften, soak up flavours of the gravy and also impart the distinct seasoned-lentil flavour to the curry. It is a complex but interesting use of lentils.

Another unusual dish that Barima preferred, especially on days when she was fasting and thus would not eat anything prepared with an onion-based masala, was cheelay ki subzi. One of the quickest curries to make, this involved pan-frying a besan pancake seasoned with green coriander and green chillies, salt and sometimes just a touch of ajwain, or carom seeds and then breaking it up into smaller bits. These were then put into a boiling gravy made simply from water seasoned with heeng, zeera and a little turmeric. The curry, apart from the basic spices, benefitted from the flavour of the soaked pancake. It was immensely enjoyable to eat it piping hot with crisp triangular parathas for an early dinner.

In the Kayasth kitchen, vegetarian food involved plenty of lentil-based dishes. Dal was also subzi, curried in many different ways, and combined with other vegetables too. This, apart from being made into snacks and the faux non-vegetarian dishes we talked about earlier. Besan, or chickpea flour, in fact was a vital ingredient in Mrs LC's kitchen and went into all sorts of preparations, cheelay ki subzi being one of them. In winter, besan could also be stuffed into big green chilli-peppers to make an instant condiment. Besan bhari mirch – always made with mustard oil – was part achaar, part subzi and a fixture on Mrs LC's winter table.

The lentil fixation is not to suggest that the family shunned vegetables altogether. Winter was cauliflower season, the singular flavour of the vegetable ensuring a delicious meal, even if it was cooked lightly. Taazi gobhi–baasi parathas (literally, fresh cauliflower–stale parathas) was a brunch combo popular with my grandparents, the field-fresh cauliflower freshly sautéed with ginger and scooped up with cold parathas made the night before. Just one of those quirky combinations someone institutionalized in the extended family.

Summer, on the other hand, meant bhindi, and parwal and torai (both varieties of gourd), all of these mixed with plenty of onions and slow-cooked till the vegetables lost all their water and what remained was the most delicious mishmash – no one bothered about texture in these instances of cooking vegetables. Torai, the quintessential Indian variety of sponge gourd, in particular, was bhunoed for so long in our house that a kilo of it would be reduced to a small bowl of chutney-like subzi. The thinnest, most tender of the variety makes for a delicious ingredient. Lucknow vendors, as late as when I was growing up in the city in the

1990s, sold them poetically as '*Laila ki ungliyan, Majnu ki pasliyan*', as thin as Laila's fingers and Majnu's ribs! In our home it was the most delicious summer special you could have and we were careful about taking tiny mouthfuls of it with much more generous helpings of dal and chawal. In winter, similar treatment was meted out to bathua, when the finely chopped leaves would be cooked with loads of garlic and slow-roasted in the kadhai till what had appeared to be more than sufficient for the entire household would be reduced to almost a quarter of its mass, and become the most prized dish on the table, with Barima strictly rationing out the helpings.

If a vegetable wasn't slow-cooked (in enough ghee or oil) for at least three-quarters of an hour in the kadhai, it was going to be no good. That was the dominant thought behind Barima's school of vegetarian cooking. Everything was laborious, but not laboured; every ingredient was cooked with a great deal of patience and attention. The stress on bhuna that dominates the clan's cooking may be quite contrary to contemporary ideas of treating ingredients lightly so that intrinsic flavours are retained, but it has some merit to it. Vegetables *do* taste much better when slow-cooked for longer, perhaps because flavours get concentrated as the water evaporates.

Chef Manu Chandra, executive chef of Olive Beach, and chef and partner, Monkey Bar and The Fatty Bao, himself from a Kayasth family, grew up on similar traditions. Even though his own approach to cooking is quite modern, he helped me understand a little bit of the kitchen chemistry that our families may have unwittingly followed and which accounted for the distinctive taste. Of course, it is entirely possible that the taste we hold up in our memory is just that of nostalgia, but processes such as the Maillard reaction are fairly well-known in the culinary world. This chemical reaction is named after the French chemist Louis-Camille Maillard, who first described it in 1912 while attempting to reproduce biological protein synthesis. Without delving into its chemistry, the Maillard reaction (between amino acids and reducing sugars) is what gives browned foods their desirable flavour. It is responsible for brown bread crusts, the golden-brown skin of roast chicken, and so on. In Kayasth khana, browning the meats to intensify flavours may follow a similar kitchen chemistry and reducing vegetables on a slow flame may lead to more complex flavour profiles coming to the fore.

Bhuna and patiently slow-cooking each dish, even the vegetarian fare, was so intrinsic to Kayasth cooking that it was a skill taught fairly early on to most girls in the family – and to those boys who wanted to dabble in the culinary arts. I certainly learned to cook vegetarian food while quite young. During the school summer vacations, the LCs and my parents would expect me to cook at least one dish for the family dinner. Mostly, I fell in with their wishes, even though it was baking that interested me then, not the laborious process of bhunna.

On my thirteenth birthday I remember turning out quite

a credible Kayasth meal albeit vegetarian. Since my mother was busy looking after my aunt who had had a baby the previous day, I cooked my entire birthday dinner for my grandparents and myself, complete with thin and evenly rounded chapattis. Mrs LC gently supervised, too ridden with arthritis to really help. It was only much later at night, when we had all fallen asleep, that my parents returned home and woke me up to the shami kebab treat they had brought along. I can still taste those kebabs in my mouth but it is really the sense of accomplishment at cooking a Kayasth meal that I wear as a badge. However, since I lack the patience to do a bhuna of everything and a sense of generosity while ladling out the ghee and masala, I am not a great cook of Kayasth khana at all. Not in the way Barima would have approved, at any rate.

There were simpler, faster dishes too, such as chunki hui matar – peas sautéed in a tempering of asafoetida. The fresh green peas were sometimes cooked with the entire pod if they were tender enough. Such dishes relied on the absolute freshness of seasonal vegetables. But a larger chunk of the cooking was much more elaborate. One of the deceptively simple, yet time-consuming recipes of the house – and indeed of all Kayasth homes, across sub-communities – is what Barima called 'margul'. I have heard other people call it, more prosaically, 'tawe par siki arvi'. The colocasia was boiled and peeled and then flattened between the palms. This would be coated with grated onions and dry masalas (including turmeric and ajwain, the classic spice to use with colocasia) and pan-fried very slowly on the tawa till the masala coating was browned and crisp.

Bharwan dishes, where you stuffed the vegetables with different ingredients to create a textural contrast and exoticize the mundane seasonal produce, were quite a favourite on Barima's table, too. While barwan karela was the overwhelming favourite, the bitter gourd stuffed with gently browned onions, bharwan tinda was also not infrequent during summer. Tinda, the Indian round gourd or apple gourd, is intrinsic to the subcontinent, one of those local vegetables that are fast disappearing under pressure from the 24×7 availability of global produce. They were also possibly the most reviled of summer squashes, deemed so plain and homely that no connoisseur of fine foods could possibly pay any attention to them.

Clearly, tinda like so many other vegetables – pumpkin, gourds like lauki, parval and assorted greens – suffers from an image problem. But the Kayasths, experts at spin-doctoring if you like, had already found ways to make these vegetables more exotic. This treatment of seasonal vegetables to long, laborious processes in order to concoct bharwan delicacies is one of the major features that distinguish the Mughal-influenced 'royal' Kayasth cooking from that of other communities in northern India. Mrs LC's recipe for bharwan tinda involved choosing the most delicate, tender fruit of the vine, scooping out the flesh from the centre and filling the space with roasted gram flour that had been seasoned with the cooling summer spices of powdered cumin, amchoor powder and fennel. The tinda would be lightly sautéed after being stuffed, resulting in one of the most delicious side dishes of the season.

The trick to bharwan karela also lay not just in choosing the right, small, raw and even-sized bitter gourd with a thin skin that would be scraped off, but also in getting the stuffing, the pyaaz ka masala right. To make this, onions would be thinly sliced into rings, *lachcha*, not conveniently and quickly chopped or grated – and then gently bhunoed with dry spices, including freshly powdered fennel and amchoor, a favourite Kayasth spice, used here to take away the bitterness. The karela meanwhile would be scraped and salted to take out the bitterness and then slit down the middle, its seeds scooped out. When the onions turned a gentle pink, they would be stuffed into the karela, the whole thing tied with a cotton thread, and then put back in the kadhai till the bitter gourd cooked and turned brown on the outside. It was a time-consuming process, the recipe a vegetarian adaption of the Muslim dolma-like recipe where minced meat is stuffed into a variety of vegetables, including all manner of gourds. Obviously, the Kayasth matriarchs cooked their vegetables as elaborately as they (or their menfolk) cooked the meats. The unravelling of these lengths of string while sitting on the dining table was a ritual of eating that was in itself symbolic of an age gone by when there was no instant gratification; the anticipation built up appetite and the journey to eating the dish was almost as delicious as the dish itself!

The pyaaz ka masala used for bharwan karela is distinctly Kayasth. It was the same masala that my ever-innovative family used to make another popular winter dish: karamkalle ke karele. If mock non-vegetarian dishes were quite the norm in the inventive Kayasth kitchen, there were as well several mock dishes to capture the experience of eating beloved vegetables not in season and thus not available. Bitter gourd, a favourite with my family and many others, is a summer vegetable in the subcontinent. In the peak of winter, my grandparents' table would see a mock karela dish: fresh and tender cabbage leaves were lightly steamed and rolled up with a stuffing of karela ka masala – the same browned onions–amchoor–powdered fennel combo. This would be lightly sautéed and presented as a delicacy. Cabbage, commonly called 'bandh gobi' in the Hindi-speaking belt, was always referred to by its Urdu name, 'karamkalla', in my grandparents home. Karamkalle ke karela was thus cabbage by another name, and taste.

Could this recipe have been referencing another Middle Eastern/Mediterranean tradition of stuffing vine leaves with mince, dolma-style? Given the syncretism evident on the Kayasth table, it is quite possible. The bharwan tradition of the subcontinent can perhaps be traced quite legitimately to the dolma dishes of the Middle East, Balkans and Central Asia. And we may have the Kayasths to thank for them.

Recipes

Bharwan Karele

These were by far the favourite summer vegetarian dish on Mrs LC's table. The balance of the fennel and amchoor flavour while spicing the filling is the key to executing the dish perfectly, as is also sourcing small, even-sized green bitter gourd.

Serves 4

INGREDIENTS

500g small, even-sized green karelas (bitter gourd)
1½ cup oil to fry
1kg onions, thinly sliced
2 tsp amchoor powder
1½ tbsp fennel powder
Salt to taste
String to tie the bitter gourd

METHOD

Scrape the karelas, slit each from the centre and take the seeds out. Rub each with salt and put on a tray placed at an angle to drain out the bitterness of the vegetable. Leave the karelas standing like this for a couple of hours.

In a kadhai, heat 1 cup oil and fry all the sliced onions till brown.

Add salt and amchoor and fennel powders to them, mixing while stirring all the time on a low flame. Add the scooped-out seeds as well (these will be only a few and tender since the karelas are young). Sauté for 5–10 minutes. This is the stuffing for the karelas.

Take the mix off the flame and cool. Stuff it into the slit bitter gourd and tie each one with string so that the masala does not fall out.

In a separate kadhai, heat about 2 tbsp of oil and gently drop the stuffed karaelas. Sauté for 5 minutes, gently turning the sides, and then cover and cook on a medium flame till the skin of the bitter gourd is cooked. This is dum cooking. The karelas will now have also changed colour to brown.

Once they are fully cooked, bhuno some more, for about 5 minutes, adding a little extra oil if necessary.

When they are nicely browned from the outside, take them off the flame. Eat with parathas or arhar dal–chawal, after unravelling the strings.

You can store the karelas in the refrigerator for a few days, taking them out a few at a time for meals.

Bharwan Bhindi

Serves 4

INGREDIENTS

3 tbsp fennel powder
2 tbsp amchoor powder
1 tsp turmeric powder

1 tbsp coriander power

Salt to taste

1kg bhindi, slit lengthwise

1 cup refined oil

A big pinch of asafoetida

METHOD

Mix all the spices (including salt), except asafoetida. Fill the slit bhindi with the mixture. Keep aside.

In a kadhai, heat ¾ of the oil and add the asafoetida.

Once it becomes aromatic, gently toss in all the stuffed bhindi. Any extra dry masala can also be added on top. Sauté for about a minute or two, then cover and cook on a low flame till the bhindi is cooked but remains firm and not mashed up.

Then, remove the lid and sauté for another 3-4 minutes, adding a little more oil if required so that the ladies' finger glistens with oil.

Serve hot with dal and rotis.

Takey Paise

This dish gets its name from the old coins of Hindustan. These are a version of the Rajasthani gatte, but are common across Kayasth homes in all regions.

Serves 4

INGREDIENTS

The 'coins'

2 cups besan (chickpea flour)

4 tbsp oil
4 tbsp onion paste
1 tsp red chilli powder
Salt to taste
4 tbsp green coriander, chopped
1 tsp garam masala
A little curd to knead this dough
1 tsp kalonji, or onion seeds
Oil for frying

The gravy

3 onions, chopped
1 tsp garlic, chopped
2 tsp ginger, chopped
Salt to taste
½ tsp turmeric powder
½ tsp red chilli powder
1 tsp coriander powder
2 tbsp yoghurt, beaten
2 tomatoes, puréed (optional)
1 cup of water
1 tbsp coriander leaves, chopped

Method

Mix the ingredients for the 'coins' and make a firm dough.

Make long cylinder shapes from this dough, half the length of your palm, and drop them in boiling water. When these float to the top, take them out with a slotted spoon. Let them cool and cut into small rounds or 'coins'.

Deep-fry till a light golden brown.

Sauté the chopped onions, ginger and garlic till golden brown.

Add the dry masalas and the beaten yoghurt, and bhuno the

masala. You can add the tomato purée (optional) for extra body and colour.

Add a cup of water and bring to a boil. Now drop the takey paise into the gravy. The final consistency should be a thick gravy.

Garnish with chopped coriander leaves.

Margul

This is a typical Kayasth preparation of colocasia, made similarly across sub-castes and regions. The trick is to slow-roast the vegetable. Owing to it being cooked on a hot flat griddle, or tawa, it is sometimes simply called 'tawe ki arvi' in other homes.

Serves 4

INGREDIENTS

1kg arvi (colocasia), boiled, peeled and flattened
500g onions, grated
20g ginger, grated
10g garlic paste
½ tsp turmeric powder
½ tsp red chilli powder
Salt to taste
200g refined oil
2 tsp ajwain (carom seeds)
1 tbsp kasoori methi (dried fenugreek leaves)

Method

Make a masala by mixing together the raw onions, ginger, garlic, turmeric, salt and red chilli powder. Smear the flattened pieces of arvi with this masala and keep aside.

On a hot plate or iron tawa, heat a little oil, roast the ajwain in it and then add the individual pieces of arvi coated with the masala. Slow-roast these on the tawa, adding oil as required, so that the arvi browns. Turn over to brown the other side. Turn off the flame.

Crush the kasoori methi in your palms and sprinkle over the arvi. Serve hot.

The ensemble caste. Weddings were big productions in the world of the LCs with their accompanying gana, bajana and khana.
(L to R) Mrs KC, Vandana Vishalakshi, Mr KC, Mrs LC, Rajeev Rishi, Beena Rishi, Sanjeev Rishi, LC, Mr PC and Mrs PC.

8

What's in the Pickle Jar?

Achaar Expertise in the Kayasth Kitchen

Much less is made of the Kayasth art of pickling than it deserves. Kayasth women may have been expert cooks of meat curries and kebabs without ever tasting the non-vegetarian ingredients, but they were equally well-known for their deft handling of achaar masalas.

Pickling of course is a form of preserving food practised the world over by almost all cultures. From the kimchi of Korea to kosher cucumber pickles, pickled herring in Scandinavia, salsas in Mexico, there are examples of pickled foods everywhere in the world. It is one of the oldest ways of treating food: two thousand years ago, when the Great Wall of China was being built, the workers apparently ate a form of sauerkraut, fermented cabbage.

Most cultures use two basic ways of pickling. The first is dunking the main ingredient in vinegar, an acid that prevents the growth of bacteria. The second common process is letting the ingredient soak in brine, a solution of salt, so that harmful bacterial growth is stemmed and the food gets fermented, changing its flavour as a result of 'good' bacterial action.

The badi-mangori tradition of making sun-dried lentil dumplings is an example of fermented food, as is the tradition of kaanji bade on Holi. Here, carrots are pickled in brine (with some mustard added in) and the lentil dumplings are left to soak in the water, furthering the process of fermentation. Kayasth women were known for making both these delicacies. But, for them 'pickling' was something entirely different. Bits of seasonal fruits and vegetables were preserved in oil and spices in a way common to many Indian communities and unique to the spice-rich subcontinent. Making spicy achaars was an art, and Kayasth women were proficient at it.

The early days of summer invariably meant at least two types of pickles being 'bottled' in huge earthen jars called *martbaans*: raw mango and jackfruit. The fruit would be diced and a strong spice mix, made at home and comprising ingredients such as amchoor powder (the prime souring agent), turmeric powder, red chilli powder and fenugreek seeds would go into the spice mix with lots of salt. This would be added to the fruit and raw, cold-pressed mustard oil poured over it all till it covered the fruit and formed a protective layer. Both the salt and the mustard oil acted as preservatives. The jar would be left out in the sun for fermentation to occur and the fruit bits to be slowly 'cooked' till neither the oil nor the fruit seemed 'raw' and all the spices had blended in.

One of the prized summer pickles in my family was the lasode ka achaar. Lasoda, a local fruit of the Indo-Gangetic plain, is a small olive-like green berry. It is intensely seasonal – available for just about fifteen days in a year. Most homes would have a shrub that gave them the required berries. Those who didn't have access to the source needed to keep a sharp watch on the local mandis and wet markets or tell the subzi-walla, the vegetable seller who came home with fresh vegetables every day, to get them a kilo or two or more of the fruit as soon as they became available. Lasode are still strictly seasonal, if at all available in the more modern markets and localities. These berries were savoured, above anything else, in summer, when our family would make lasode ki subzi, a favourite of Mrs LC's, and more importantly, lasode ka achaar, to be made, stored, distributed only to a choice few and consumed discerningly over subsequent months.

The sour karonde, pinkish local berries tinier than the round, green lasode, was the monsoon equivalent of the lasode. Most homes had a shrub of this berry too. Karonde, supremely tart, were made into a 'fresh pickle' – sautéed with green chillies and ginger (two traditionally 'warming' ingredients apt for the rain, according to Ayurveda), or put in a lime solution with these two ingredients – and used as a table condiment.

The tradition of 'fresh' condiments or side dishes was

quite strong, too. Summer meant freshly sautéed aam ki launji – ripe mango chopped up and tempered with kalonji seeds and red chillies, with a little sugar thrown in for a burst of sweet–salt–sour umami. Else, roasted eggplant would be pummelled into cooling yoghurt, topped with chopped onions, garlic and fresh coriander leaves. It was not a thin raita but a replacement for the usual thick yoghurt on the table. In winter, when the big, fat, not-so-hot green chillies came to the local markets, they were stuffed with roasted gram flour and lightly sautéed in mustard oil, adding another dimension to a meal.

The winter pickle to look forward to was not the gobi–gajar–shalgam (cauliflower–carrots–turnips), the staple of Punjabi homes. Instead, the UP Kayasths turned to red chillies stuffed with fennel and amchoor, and pickled in mustard oil. The famous lal mirch ka achaar from Banaras is modelled on these lines. This was the pickle that accompanied mathris, the fried flour discs favoured as evening snacks.

Though Mrs LC would sit majestically at the dining table, mixing spices for red chilli, mango or lasode pickles, it was Mrs Bishen Swaroop, my maternal grandmother, Naniji, who was the acknowledged and esteemed pickle-putter of the family. Her sense of measure and balance while pickling was deemed perfect. The lime pickle she made was legendary; it was entirely without oil, just spices and salt and the acidity of the lime doing the trick. This was stored away, the flavour intensifying with every passing year, and finally giving us the blackened pickled limes that became ever more prized as their antiquity and flavour increased. If the best of red wine ages well, so did my maternal grandmother Naniji's pickles, and rarely did her achaar spoil. That must have undoubtedly been due to her experience and talent with spices and oil. But both Barima and Naniji had strict rituals surrounding achaar. The achaar was to be mixed with 'clean' hands, post a bath. Once made, no menstruating woman was allowed to even touch the martbaan. It was their belief that such a touch would immediately ruin the pickle. It was one of those irrational beliefs that ruled the Hindu Kayasth inner kitchens; certain foods and certain people were treated as ritually pure or impure. Liberal education for women, the seemingly relaxed mores and adopted manners, first of the Mughal elite and then the English colonial rulers, could not change these inherited, deeply entrenched patterns and beliefs.

With the arrival of the British, as the educated Kayasths switched sides to enter the portals of power in the new colonial set-up, the dining table made an appearance in many Kayasth homes. But it would be quite some time before the inner status quo would be challenged. Like the symbol it was of the outer masculine world of material success and manners, the dining table remained in the 'outer' dining rooms, used by men primarily to entertain high-ranking sahibs. As Kayasth men increasingly adapted to the changing cultural mores and imbibed more of the power of the Raj, this symbol of progress and superiority became an integral part of their lifestyle. These men (and some women) changed their social behaviour and eating rituals, once again. But as in the days of Mughal power, when eating meat had become quite the norm in Kayasth homes, along with literacy in Urdu and wearing fine white muslin kurta–pyjama, the change remained, in many ways superficial.

The inner world – of pickles, of the belief in the 'purity' of foods, of religious rituals – remained traditional. It was a world dominated by Kayasth women, who in northern India remained true to their mainly Vaishnavite moorings. They went to the newly established English schools, earned their degrees, picked up some of the manners of the rulers, but nevertheless remained rooted in an earlier world. It would take many more years for that to change.

Recipes

Kaanji

Kaanji bade, where small lentil dumplings are pickled in water spiked with mustard, is quite the Kayasth special around Holi. In the home of the LCs no one really cared much for it. Instead, my mother put the prettier looking carrot kanji. For my food promotions and pop-up dinners, I serve this beautiful red in a wine glass.

Serves 4

INGREDIENTS

1kg carrot, cut into batons
1 beetroot, cut into small pieces
50g rai (small red mustard seeds), ground with a little water
1 small piece of gur (jaggery)
2–3 litres of water
Salt to taste

METHOD

Wash the carrots and the beetroot and lightly boil in enough water (about 2–3 litres should be enough). Cool. Now, add the rai, salt and gur. Leave it to pickle for about six to seven days.

Lasode ka Achar

Quite the summer delicacy in Kayasth homes, lasode, or 'Indian cherry' as it is sometimes called, is a highly seasonal fruit, available for just about fifteen days in a year between April end and May. The green unripe fruit, which resembles an olive, was used to make both a vegetable preparation as well as this pickle in Mrs LC's home.

INGREDIENTS

1kg green lasode
Salt to taste
500g mustard oil
5 raw mangoes, peeled
1 tbsp turmeric powder
3 tbsp fennel powder
2 tbsp red chilli powder
2 tbsp vinegar

METHOD

Lightly boil the lasode in water with a little salt and 2 tbsp oil. Make sure they remain firm and al dente but soften just enough to remove the pit.

Lightly steam the raw mango, remove the pulp and mix this with turmeric, fennel and red chilli powders, salt and vinegar.

This is the stuffing for the lasode that have been pitted. Once the berries are filled, smear them with a little oil and leave them for a day in a martabaan, or earthen jar.

Then top up the martabaan with the rest of the oil. Leave to pickle in the sun for 4–5 more days. Store.

9

Fasting, Feasting

Weddings, Festivals and Special

What were the desserts on Mrs LC's table? Barima was quite fond of meetha, and would often reprimand me for putting far too little sugar in any dessert I attempted. I was never very keen on Indian desserts. The family had put me through all the standard lessons in baking and even ice-cream making. But I collected dessert recipes right through my adolescence, cooking in the dead of the night – my preferred work hours – while the rest of the family slept. LC, who was partial to 'Western' cakes and bakes, would receive the results of all those experiments, from basic pound cakes to 'pineapple surprise', most enthusiastically.

Mrs LC, on the other hand, definitely preferred her traditional mithai. One of my favourite memories is of her going on morning walks with us, her five grandchildren. On the way back home we would stop at a neighbourhood halwai shop, and she would ask us to choose one mithai each for ourselves to begin the day with. It became our summer holiday routine, this exposure to the overly sweet world of Indian mithai, as each of us strove to do better than the other in making an 'exotic' choice. It could be balushahi one day, paan ki gilori another, kheer kadam, shaped and coloured like an egg but made with *chhena* (curd cheese) the next. The variety seemed endless in those days, as did our entertainment.

At home, however, dessert choices were far more limited. One of the best-known Kayasth specials from old Delhi was lauki ki lauj, a dish that Kayasth matriarchs had in common with their Baniya counterparts. This was made with bottle gourd grated coarsely and then cooked in milk with an almost negligible amount of khoya. When the milk thickened and the lauki got pulped into a sludge, you could set it on a thali and cut squares or diamonds out of it, sprinkling just some cardamom powder for scent. In our UP home, however, lauki ki lauj was never made. Our special dessert was Barima's gajar ka halwa, made similarly, with the addition of raisins and cashews. It is all the more special for me as it often formed part of my childhood bedtime ritual, Barima narrating the recipe to me as I nodded off.

My mother's speciality, on the other hand, has been kheer, rice pudding, whose exceptional taste belies the simplicity of the recipe. It remains a must-have party dessert. Suji ka halwa and meethe paratha stuffed with sugar were the more everyday desserts. And though my grandparents always sought something sweet after every meal – sometimes home-made besan barfi or besan laddo, at other times gazak, a winter confection ordered from Meerut – the Kayasth dessert repertoire definitely seems less formidable than that for other kinds of dishes.

Festivals were really the time when meetha came into its own. From gujjas to pue to makhane ki kheer, different sweets were marked out for different rituals. In the home of the LCs these were made diligently, ritualistically, every year, regardless of whether they were popular goodies for the family or not.

With Barima insisting that all festivals be celebrated together by the extended family, whichever son's house was Mr and Mrs LC's base at the time of a festival became the focal point for the entire clan. Aunts, uncles and cousins would travel great distances to come to our home for any festival that Barima and Papa were celebrating with us. There was chaos, confusion, cooking and eating competitions, and life was a party despite the many squabbles that erupted among us. Of the many festivals the family celebrated together with gusto, Holi was my favourite. It would start off with a Rang Paashi dinner, before the actual festival of colours. This was the first evening when trays of freshly made gujjas stuffed with khoya, chironji seeds and raisins, kishmish – that Holi staple – were brought out. We would begin by ritually 'worshipping' the food with a little ceremonial gulal before the Scotch was brought out and the khana–peena began in earnest.

The evening would kick off with a cultural *mehfil*, soiree

of sorts, depending on the scale of the dinner. But even if it was an intimate family affair, it was quite common for traditional holis to be sung by both men and women. Harmoniums and tablas were brought out, diaries containing lyrics dusted off and pored over, and songs sung with spirit and fervour. More creative types would use the audience for a spot of shayari, or *hasya kavita* (comic verse) narration, all penned by themselves. At the beginning of the evening, a little gulal would be put on everyone, particularly the in-laws. The evening, after all, was specially dedicated to sons-in-law and daughters-in-law, who would symbolically cross the boundaries of social sobriety and 'smear' (it was only a respectful tikka on the forehead) their in-laws with colour.

The Rang Paashi dinner was elaborate: a couple of meat curries, pulao, kebabs and, of course, vegetarian fare served up with pooris and kachoris. The breads themselves would often be coloured – spinach, beetroot and other such natural ingredients kneaded into the dough – to fit in with the larger Holi theme. On the other hand, the Holi lunch itself was quite simple. For one, quite surprisingly, this was a strictly vegetarian affair. But first there were the snacks for the morning festivities – kaanji (pickled carrot water fermented with mustard seeds), namakpare and various home-made cold chaats like dahi bade and dahi papdi – apart from bhang, or marijuana leaves, in thandai and in laddoos. All this was in keeping with smash-sobriety, break-boundaries spirit of Holi, during which spraying others with coloured water, playing pranks and fun foods were institutionalized jests. Tired after the games, we would troop into the dining room for a pretty standard lunch: taazi gobi, baasi parathas. The cauliflower, the last of the season, would be freshly sautéed with ginger and eaten with stale parathas made the night before. There would also be crispy fried papdi and melt-in-the-mouth dahi bade made by my mother, spiced with just roasted and powdered cumin seeds and a tangy saunth. Holi in my mind is forever made up of these contrasting flavours – but none more so than the smell and flavour of freshly fried gujjas.

In the home of the LCs, we never called them gujiya, like most of India did. Like the samosa, gujja or gujiya is probably a fusion dish. If sambusak or the spanakopita is a predecessor of the samosa, filo pastry from the Greek/ Middle East and Balkan traditions transformed into the gujiya too when it travelled to India – fried instead of baked, thicker maida shells replacing the thin sheets. The filling is quite another matter. The gujiya is one of those perplexing Indian dishes common throughout the subcontinent whose recipe changes every few hundred kilometres. From the pedakiyas of Bihar to the kajikayalu of Andhra, karanji of Maharashtra and nevries of Goa, everyone does the snack in bewilderingly different ways, stuffing into the shell anything from dry coconut to roasted semolina, cashews, raisins, khoya and more. Nowadays sugar syrup and a coating of a few strands of saffron sometimes jazz up the festive staple when it retails out of fancier sweet shops.

Barima – and indeed my entire family – would be disdainful of these 'other', particularly bazaar-bought, versions. A true gujja in my home was and remains a fairly simple affair: khoya is mixed with sugar, raisins and chironji (no other nuts are permitted in the filling), with a dash of green cardamom powder. The snobbish way to eat a gujja at home was always when it was piping hot, fresh off the kadhai. The aroma of the slightly caramelized khoya can be addictive in the same way as the smell of freshly baked bread is.

Gujjas were often paired with the other Holi special, a uniquely Mathur Kayasth festive snack, papdi – besan papads rolled out very thin and fried in mustard oil. It made for a great sweet and savoury combination. These papdis are not the small chaat disks of refined flour that most people associate with the term. Instead, these are more like papads, but fried fresh instead of sun-baked. To call a papdi 'papad' – something that many first-timers to our festive fare were guilty of – was a big insult. Barima instantly looked down upon anyone who didn't have the cultural sophistication to appreciate the difference!

If gujjas were an annual ritual, the making of papdi was a biennial must. It was a snack to be feasted upon during the winter festivities of Diwali as well, the other major festival of our world. Like everything else, the festival of lights came with its own carefully calibrated rituals of feasting. On the day of the main Lakshmi Puja, before the crackers gifted to us by our grandparents could be burst,

Barima would gather the family for a puja of sixty-four lit diyas. This was different from how we had worshipped the unlit, 'cold' lamps a night before, on Chotti Diwali, before settling down to games of teen patti, the only time the children were allowed to play cards. On Badi Diwali, the main night, mustard oil was filled in each earthen lamp and they were all lit. Kheel and batashas, puffed rice and sugar confections, were the ritualistic offerings made to these lit lamps – perhaps a homage to the bounty of the earth, both rice and sugar cane being freshly harvested in autumn in northern India. And then Barima would tell us the Diwali story.

It is a myth retold through generations. I am not sure how old the story is but it is likely that this is a version that emerged relatively later, with the cult of the misogynistic Tulsi Ramayana and other texts, where older rituals and stories became mixed up with morality tales and social commentary rooted in an increasingly aggressive and reactionary feudal order. The story goes like this: one Diwali night in Ayodhya, Lakshmi finds only a single house unlit. So instead of visiting the other shining mansions, she decides, for a change, to visit the poor old man's darkened hut. As she is about to step inside, the wily old man blocks her way, kicks her away. On being questioned by the goddess of wealth, he abuses and kicks her, calling her a whore who is fickle in her affections. Only when Lakshmi promises to stay in his house for seven generations is she given permission to enter. The story ends with the family praying that, Lakshmi favour their home too for seven generations like she did the old man's household.

It's an offensive, violent story. But as children, we not only accepted it as a ritualistic piece but also found the profanities coming out of my grandmother's mouth entertaining. There was never any questioning of the misogynistic morality tale; the abused Lakshmi tamely stayed put in our home, and we wound up the Diwali festivities. Not with fireworks – that was just the interlude – but with a late dinner of yams and pooris. Zimikand, or yam, curried in a thick gravy, was a must-eat on Diwali night – even more than the assortment of rich sweets and savouries, kaju katli and besan papdi that had been prepared at home for the festival. The zimikand would be diligently scraped clean, fried – lest a rogue piece cause the throat to itch – and then slow-cooked in yoghurt before being simmered in a thick onion-based gravy. Almost meat-like in its texture, it was eaten with pooris.

This was the dish we associated with the night of Lakshmi Puja – a ritual dish consumed because it was believed that Lakshmi resided in the plant, a hardy tuber that propagates easily and hence associated with fertility and wealth. Eating a food to imbibe its 'magical' properties is, of course, an ancient ritual across communities, particularly agrarian ones. Gold and silver varq, for instance, coat several sweets in India even today, in a continuation of an ancient trend where bits of these noble metals were added to foods across cultures, including the Chinese and the European (during the Renaissance) to provide vitality, offer protection from disease, and ensure affluence and authority to the people who ate them. Coconut and betel are symbols of fertility and hence consumed during weddings and similar rituals. We children, of course, did not understand the symbolism behind zimikand. We just knew the ritual of eating it every Diwali night. In any case, it was a delicious preparation. Everything was polished off, both the food and the stories.

Did the LCs' household ever fast? Not really, is the simple answer. But then fasting in the family was never a simple matter of not eating. Not eating particular kinds of food was acceptable if more exciting alternatives had been found. One of our favourite festivals was Janmashtami precisely for this reason. The birth of Krishna had to be celebrated with lots of doodh and dahi, quite naturally in the Hindi heartland, and also strictly vegetarian fare. A large number of Kayasths, especially families from Delhi, Agra and western UP, have typically been devotees of Lord Krishna, also called Bihariji. This was one festival where even the Kayasths didn't eat meat, honouring the cowherd deity, protector of cattle and men. What we ate on the day of the fast was quite a divine meal at any rate.

The morning would kick-start with phalahar, literally a fruit (no grain) meal, but the breakfast included not just cut fruit but fried nuts, groundnuts in particular, and lotus seed. Lunch comprised the no-grain kootu (buckwheat flour), pooris and a potato curry flavoured with just green chillies, ginger and asafoetida; no turmeric powder was used in vrat ka khana, or fasting food. But the highlight of the meal undoubtedly was makhane ki kheer. The kheer was indulgently made. There was no skimping on the chironji, makhane and raisins that went into the milk, thickened so that the consistency was not that of a sludge but liquid that you drank out of bowls. My mother, the family's expert at making all kinds of milk puddings, turned out the best makhane ki kheer that we preferred over rice pudding any day. But it was only during Janmashtami that this particular dessert was made and eaten.

Barima, on the other hand, was known for her charnamrit. A ritualistic offering of five 'uncooked' and hence pure ingredients – unboiled milk, curd, honey, tulsi leaf and ganga jal – charnamrit, or panchamrit (a mixture of five nectars) as it is also called, was part of the prasad offered to the deities after every puja, including the midnight Janmashtami celebration. After the deities had ostensibly had their sip, we drank it by the glassful. Not for this family – one strictly devoted to food – was the custom of having a single drop or two in the cup of the palm. For us charnamrit was much more than a ritual. It was perhaps our favourite beverage! As children we fought over the last glass.

Pagi hui mewa, dry fruits and nuts roasted in ghee coated in caramelized sugar, was the distinct prasad prepared only on Janmashtami. As a ritualistic offering, it is still a fixture in both Kayasth and Baniya homes in UP. In the LCs' home, the guidelines for making it were quite well defined: we never mixed up the dried fruit. Instead, separate plates were prepared with chironji, kharbooze ke beej (melon seeds) and grated dry coconut, all 'pagi hui' – each ingredient roasted in ghee – before sugar and a hint of water were added to coat these in a thin layer of sweetness. Basically, they were candied nuts, but the layer of sugar was subtle and the flavour of the nuts stood out. Chironji was the family favourite. The pagi hui mewa would be stored and kept away for an instant energy-boosting snack or dessert for days after the monsoon festival.

Also part of the prasad was kasar, which the rest of the world, primarily the Punjabi-speaking one, calls panjiri. Barima would make kasar lovingly, adding plenty of ghee to the kadhai and then roasting atta in it till it began to give off a rich fragrance. Powdered sugar would then be added to the flour and finally a few tulsi leaves – to impart holiness to the preparation. There was no dried fruit and no other additive but the kasar had a distinct flavour, slightly smoky, because it had been kept near the ritualistic diya at the altar or the fire of a havan. And this is what piety or, well, purity tastes like to me till today!

The other day devoted to Krishna and hence totally vegetarian even for the Kayasths was the Annakoot ki puja. Part of the Diwali festivities – observed two days after the main Lakshmi Puja – Annakoot was distinct because fifty-six types of food offerings (called chhappan bhog) were made to Lord Krishna, protector of the earth and its bounties, symbolized by the story of the cowherd god lifting the mountain Govardhan like a giant umbrella to protect people and cattle from Indra's wrath when the king of the celestial demi-gods caused rain to lash the land.

Typically, the feast comprised both cooked and uncooked foods, including seasonal fruits and vegetables. If there was an agrarian festival that the relatively urbanized Kayasths used to observe, it is this. There would also be different kinds of poori, fried leafy greens, varieties of mithai, as also things like paan, cloves, elaichi, all auspicious spices or symbolic foods in the Hindu world view. In the big Kayasth families, some of which were also landed, only daughters-in-law cooked the feast, with the assistance of eight or ten members of the domestic staff. Since the LCs' family had become urbanized fairly early in its history, Annakoot was never a big occasion for us. It is only later that I learned of its significance, on meeting other families, particularly the large joint families, whose food memories include the astonishing number of dishes prepared on that day.

I have talked about the big feast on Dussehra, when the kaliya would make an appearance on our table. This was post the stringent Navratras in autumn, during which for nine days families would fast (though the LCs' family was never quite strict about this, we eschewed meat and eggs during this time). The period of symbolic penance ended with the fireworks of Ravana being burnt, Rama returning victorious and kaliya reemerging on our table. The good had triumphed and good times had resumed. All was well with the world and, to mark that, it was fitting that meat should be cooked.

By far the strictest fast that Barima and her bahus undertook was the Karva Chauth. These were the pre-Karan Johar days, and Karva Chauth was hardly a glamorous event in the Hindu festive calendar. Many Kayasth families skipped it entirely. Some women fasted but drank a glass or two of milk for nourishment during the day. Barima, however, was strict and traditional about it. This was the day that she and her daughters-in-law spent not only without food but, more importantly, without even a sip of water – and this arduous task was undertaken with minimum fuss.

The women would wake up pre-sunrise and have a sensible *sargai*, or breakfast, of toast with butter, tea, sometimes even fried egg, and betel leaf. The paan was the only thing that was ritualistic, perhaps to keep the throat moist through the day. They ate and drank nothing the rest of the day. When the moon finally rose, the women went up the terrace of the house, offered the moon god water, pooris and pue and finally ate bits of these in the presence of their husbands, for whose long life they had been praying.

In patriarchal Hindu society, the burden of the husband's well-being and longevity has always been placed on the woman – and her virtuousness. That is really what Karva Chauth is all about – a day celebrating the devotion of the wife to the husband. The anxiety which this narrative provoked in women was quite perceptible in the LCs' home too. Barima was quite strict about when all the 'suhaag' paraphernalia – symbols of a woman's married status – was bought. Things like toe rings that married women wear, gold jewellery or even simple cosmetics like bindis and vermillion that women of that generation routinely used in the parting of their hair could only be purchased on set auspicious days of the lunar calendar that Hindu homes, including those of the Kayasths, followed to mark out festivals.

When LC was about to go to the hospital for a surgery – one from which he would never recover – Mrs LC, the strangely intuitive person that she was, began to inexplicably lose her symbols of suhaag. Her bindi fell off in the bath, her toe rings went missing, her bangles cracked. From these portents she gleaned that the end was near, even though no one had told her how life-threatening the surgery was. People living together and deeply connected with each other perhaps experience such phenomena. But for my grandmother, this was also possibly the result of lifelong anxieties related to rituals and symbols around a woman's marital status that she had internalized. Karva Chauth only reaffirmed this anxiety to keep that status intact. The fast was so sacrosanct that a married woman had to necessarily keep it every year, if she started it once, with not a drop of water going down her throat even under extreme circumstances lest it provoked the wrath of the gods.

In a dire emergency, the fast could be transferred, however, with the husband fasting in lieu of the wife. In my grandparents' patriarchal world, this was strangely quite acceptable. What was also acceptable was the laissez-faire meal at the end of the fast. Usually, religious fasts are ended with a simple, Sattvic, or 'pure', no-onion-no-garlic meal. In the LCs' home, even though the strict ritualistic austerity of Karva Chauth was mandatorily observed, the latter half of the Sattvic tradition seems to have been abandoned. At the end of the day, the food cooked was rich fare, including even non-vegetarian food, some kebabs or kaliya with pooris.

This seems to have been a feature in many other Kayasth homes. My friend Abhishek Hajela, a travel photographer whose origins are in Agra, recalls that his mother and taijis, aunts, would end their fast with a meal of pooris and kofte – not vegetarian kofte, but those made with mince! That is the Karva Chauth dish in his family home. Just like kaliya–kachori is my home's Dussehra dish. At the LCs', while there were no fixed rules to end the fast, there was one mandatory sweet that the women bit into and in fact offered to the mythic goddesses who emerged from the moon in the legend related to Karva Chauth, protectors of their marital status: pue – sweet wholewheat fritters, sweetened with sugar and deep-fried. The women first offered bits of pue and water to the moon and the godesses and then took a long, deep sip themselves, along with the sweet, to bring all austerities to an end.

Recipes

Pue

These are sweet flour fritters made on Karva Chauth. The fast ended with a bite of these.

Makes about 20 small dumplings

INGREDIENTS

1 cup atta (wholewheat flour)

¾ cup sugar

½ tsp green cardamom powder

Water to make a thin batter

Oil for frying

METHOD

Mix all the dry ingredients, add water and make a thin batter. Let it rest for about 30 minutes.

Heat oil in a kadhai. When it is smoking hot, drop in a little batter at a time with a spoon to make small, round fritters.

Hot pue can be had with vanilla ice cream too!

Makhane ki Kheer

This is fasting food, made in our family only on Janamashtami. The kheer is not really a dessert; it is served together with kuttu ki poori and aloo. Makhana, the seed of a water lily, is common fasting food in north india.

INGREDIENTS

250g makhana
1 tbsp ghee
50g raisins
2kg milk
50g chironji
500g sugar
100g green cardamoms, crushed

METHOD

Split all the makhana in half and dry-roast in a pan with ghee.

Soak the raisins in warm water for 10 minutes.

Boil milk on a slow flame for around 10 minutes or till it thickens.

Add the roasted makhana, chironji seeds and raisins, and boil for another 10 minutes.

Remove from heat, add sugar and stir well to dissolve. Garnish with crushed cardamom.

Charnamrit

Literally 'the elixir from the lord's feet', charnamrit – or panchamrit as it is also called because it involves the mixing of five uncooked ingredients – is a ritualistic drink. In the home of the LCs, it was made as part of every major puja as prasad. But it became a gourmet delight for the family. It had to be made in large quantities because all of us drank several glasses of it. Mrs LC herself made it. The ingredients were mixed together by *andaaz*, instinct, and since this was part of the prasad one couldn't taste to check. Miraculously, however, the andaaz never went wrong. The charnamrit, the ritualistic offering that it is cannot be made without a few drops of water from the river Ganga. Ganga jal, or water from the river, used to traditionally be stored in cans in homes for various cleaning and ritual purification purposes.

Ingredients

- 1kg milk, unboiled, cold
- 250g yoghurt
- 1tsp honey
- 250g powdered sugar
- A few tulsi leaves
- 5 types of mewa, or dried fruit
- 20g chironji
- 20g raisins
- 20g makhana
- A few dry coconut slivers
- 2 pieces of chuhara, a big raisin
- A few drops of Gangajal (water from the Ganga, considered to be holy)

Method

Mix everything together. Make sure that the sugar has dissolved. Chill and serve.

10

Pyala and Hala

The Kayastha Fondness for Scotch

मैं कायस्थ कुलोदभव मेरे पुरखों ने इतना ढ़ाला,
मेरे तन के लोहू में है पचहत्तर प्रतशित हाला,
पुशतैनी अधकिार मुझे है मदरिालय के आँगन पर,
मेरे दादों परदादों के हाथ बकिी थी मधुशाला।

– Harivansh Rai Bachchan, *Madhushala*

Kayastha am I, my forebears shaped me so
That my blood is three-fourths intoxicant;
The garden of the tavern is my ancestral right;
It was my forefathers, after all, who traded away the drinkery.

Neither Diwali nor Holi or any other festivity or celebration in my family was ever complete without some, if not copious, amounts of alcohol. To drink was to celebrate life. It was an 'auspicious' ritual of plenty.

I did not think much of the uniqueness of this tradition till I grew up and started writing on food history. In the

Indian context, where a great deal of hypocrisy exists with regard to alcohol and its consumption, where so many communities frown upon it, and where surreptitious 'car-o-bars' are almost institutionalized, for a community to have alcohol firmly ensconced as a social tradition – almost like the European set-up where drinking wine, in particular, is a way of life – is very unusual indeed. But even a cursory look at the history of the Kayasths immediately gives us some very firm foundations for the establishment of this convention.

It is known that many Mughal royals were fond of their wine, despite religious injunctions in Islam against drinking of any alcohol. Jahanara Begum, Shah Jahan's favourite eldest daughter, the wielder of much power, a follower of Sufism and an iconoclast by all accounts, was so fond of drinking (Shiraz wine) that she is described in some accounts as 'barely able to stand'. It is easy to conjecture that Kayasths, the educated elite, close confidants of the Mughal aristocrats, began to share this taste for alcohol, perhaps after initially using it as a tool for social bonding. With the rise of British imperialism, as the Kayasths adapted to changing ways of life, their alcohol preference too seems to have changed, from wine and other local liqueurs distilled for Mughal royalty and upper classes to whisky. The home of the LCs, like all Kayasth homes, always had a bottle or two of good quality (and real) Scotch at hand. These were usually brought out only on special occasions – on festivals or during an evening gathering of the extended family. No

Kayasth celebration was complete without some good old Scotch, and Rang Paashi in particular – which occurred two days before Holi – was an evening dedicated completely to nursing a glass of whisky over music.

'You know, you must begin the chapter (on whiskey) with those lines from *Madhushala*,' says my lively friend Amrita, with whom I have connected after a very long time. A sharp litigations lawyer, she spends her days in the Supreme Court and brings the same sense of purpose to our forays at eating out. Both of us love food, and both of us love our wine. It is only later that we discover our Kayasth connection – she belongs to a well-known Kayasth family from UP – which adds yet another dimension to this friendship.

In school, a few *rubaii*s, or quatrains, from *Madhushala* were part of my curriculum. This mellifluous, highly metaphorical work, which catapulted Dr Harivansh Rai Bachchan to instant poetic fame as the leading light of Hindi literature's Chhayawadi movement, found quite a resonance with my Kayasth brain and blood. The main motif through all the quatrains of the poem is *hala*, or alcohol. The choice may have been surprising at a time when Bachchan's contemporaries were writing on nationalism, nature and such. But it is unsurprising when you consider not just the Sufi–mystical influence on the poet but also his Kayasth pedigree, the fact that he was the product of an inclusive, more liberal culture less bound by religious conventions.

Madhushala is a classic. Its deep sense of rhythm and its complex philosophic underpinnings are unmatched in the corpus of Indian literature. It is reminiscent of Omar Khayyam's widely popular, evocative, twelfth-century *Rubaiyaat* that Bachchan was to later translate. Though Bachchan's stature as a literary genius grew with the publishing of *Madhushala*, he also became forever associated with *pyala* (cup) and hala (alcohol).

My grandfather, LC, also a native of Allahabad like Bachchan and many other Kayasth families, and a man of some talent when it came to *tuk bandi*, or rhyming, closely identified with both the persona and the works of Harivansh Rai Bachchan. He never failed to point out how this talented poet eventually lost out to the likes of the more identifiably nationalistic bards like Maithili Sharan Gupt, when it came to being tagged India's 'national poet'. For LC, given to enjoying nazm and ghazals, forms of Urdu verse, with as many references to drinking as lost love, and not above penning instant, funny verse with scatological references, obviously 'serious' content was never a measure of poetic talent. Bachchan for him remained the tallest bard – that he was writing about the pyala and *saki bala* (a young woman as the cupbearer) to talk about life was only a measure of his sophistication.

I picked up the poem again quite recently, after Amrita's injunction. As I went through the deeply rhythmic work, enjoying the shape of the words as much as their sound and meaning, I was struck anew by how unusual it must have been in 1935, with the national discourse being shaped by Gandhiji's abstemious morality in an India preparing for independence, to have bucked that trend and not written something idealistic or jingoistic. Only a person of Bachchan's background could have made sublime poetry out of wine. The Cambridge-educated poet was quite cosmopolitan, as a reading of his life suggests. Nevertheless, when in the above rubaii he pays obeisance to his caste, saying that even though he himself is not a drinker he has been able to write *Madhushala* thanks to his Kayasth forefathers, because of whom he has 75 per cent alcohol in his blood – we cheer him on. After all, the poet is stating the literal truth! Alcohol has indeed always been part of the Kayasth bloodline.

Both Amrita and I instinctively recognize this soft spot for alcohol. Like Bachchan, we may not drink that much or that regularly, but alcohol is quite definitely in our bloodlines. We are sitting at La Bodega, a Mexican restaurant in Delhi. The tacos de pescado are pretty decent but the wine is off. So we switch to margaritas – and talk Scotch. The Kayasth fascination with scotch is legendary. Scotch and shami kebab could, in fact, be the metaphor for an entire way of life that is now practically lost to the forces of globalization. If the enduring image of Wajid Ali Shah, Lucknow's last nawab, is of dancing and playing chess as the British took away his kingdom, the affluent Kayasth babu or landlord is frozen in time with his evening's chhota peg and kebab. How did the Kayasths become so devoted to their Scotch and soda? How did Chivas Regal, Cutty Sark or Black Label become so revered among a community of scribes?

Though India has always had local drinking traditions amongst different communities (flower- and fruit-based local brews like the toddy or mahua liquor are still consumed), the general consensus is that there is no tradition of drinking in the country and that alcohol is in some way contrary to something sweepingly defined as 'Indian culture'. This is ironical because early texts all mention brewing, which was very much prevalent in ancient India. The *Arthashastra*, for instance, has twelve stray references to alcohol and even the Ramayana has four. From these references, historians contend that different types of alcohol were permitted among different castes: while the 'lower castes' drank grain-based brews, the 'upper castes' like the Kshatriyas were permitted flower- or fruit-based alcohol. Only the Brahmins didn't drink. In fact, according to the food historian K.T. Achaya, even in the Ramayana, the epic that binds various subcultures in India and is so revered, Sita – the blameless heroine, now worshipped as a goddess – was offered *maireya* by Rama; this appears to have been a fruit- or flower-based distilled liquor popular with royalty at the time.

Reformist movements like Buddhism and Jainism changed some of these cultural mores, and alcohol, not permitted by Islam, must have become a further taboo for the common people at least by the time of the medieval Muslim rule. However, the Muslim nobility, right from the Sultanate period (thirteenth century), did consume wine. The 'first Mughal', Babur, alternated between bingeing on alcohol (and bhang) that he drank out of his gold or silver goblets, and total abstinence when he would break the cups, writes K.T. Achaya in *A Historical Dictionary of Indian Food*. Jahangir would consume almost twenty cups of double-distilled alcohol by the end of his days, and though Aurangzeb enforced prohibition, later-day Mughals like the *sada rangila*, eternally colourful, Mohammad Shah were undoubtedly patrons as much of wine as of the arts. During Mohammad Shah's reign, for instance, Urdu, qawwali, sarod, legendary courtesans, music and dance flourished, never mind the interruptions to hedonistic pleasure-seeking in Shahjahanabad by the invasions of Nadir Shah, who carried away the Koh-i-Noor. Rangila, in fact, is just a synonym for shaukeen – men of leisure in pursuit of pleasure – the epithet Kayasths too have always found attached to them. Drinking, as well as the interest in poetry and music, was a gift from the Muslim nobility, imbibed into the cultural fabric by the Kayasths with their usual enthusiasm for anything new. The drink of choice changed when the British introduced Scotch to India in the nineteenth century. With the change in political power, Kayasths switched sides. The adaptability ingrained in the literate community meant that members were quick to adapt to the new language of the colonial masters, English. And, as before, language became a vehicle for other cultural nuances to find their way into the life of the Kayasths. From wine and other local, brews preferred by the Muslim nobility, the Kayasths switched to Scotch.

It is debatable whether India's first distillery was set up

in Kanpur or Kasauli. There are different claims, but we do know that these distilleries came up in the early part of the nineteenth century, set up by ex-East India Company soldiers with Scottish links, who were missing their 'water of life' in the new, much hotter country. The distilleries were modelled on those in Scotland: Edward Dyer, who set up the Kasauli brewery in 1821, before the cantonment town was established, brought the equipment for brewing and distilling from that country. And the seeds for India's love affair with whisky were sown.

This whisky was embraced by both the Army and the host of civil servants (with only British officers initially peopling its top ranks) trained to govern the jewel in the crown. Gradually, by the turn of the twentieth century, as a handful of Indians – many of them educated, English-literate Kayasths – began to make it to the upper echelons of the elite Indian Civil Service, the cult of drinking Scotch grew amongst them too. It may have been just one of those customs initially acquired by the fledgling babus. But it grew – fast – to become a deeply entrenched cultural practice.

If drinking in India is frowned upon in general, women who drink are viewed with even more disapproval. It is less so in the metros, but stereotypes persist and women who frequent bars and pubs have often enough been harassed by custodians of 'Indian cultural values'. On the other hand, it is socially quite acceptable for Kayasth women to habitually drink, and many do. On Holi, Diwali and other festivals, when there has always been free-flowing alcohol, it remains a custom for the women of the house to be offered drinks of their choice – beer, gin-and-tonic, wine, stiff whisky, whatever may take their fancy.

'I am so glad I grew up in a family where I did not have to hide the fact that I was drinking,' remarks Amrita, as we sit sipping our margaritas, debating whether the Cointreau in it has been substituted for a cheaper liqueur. 'I have seen so many friends hide their alcohol in Pepsi, drink surreptitiously. My first drink was made by my uncle,' she declares. 'And my mother's by my grandfather,' I retort. My own first sips of alcohol almost certainly came from the glasses that my father, uncles or grandfather nursed, because it was also considered *laad*, a sign of affection, to give small sips of one's drink to younger members of the family.

When my mother got married and came to my father's home for the first time, a ru-nu-maii ritual was performed as usual. The term means 'unveiling'; the Urdu word also points to the mixed Indo-Islamic heritage of the Kayasths – marriage rituals are replete with such references. The new bride was the centre of this ceremony, where all the family elders would gather, see her face and give her a gift of jewellery. The ru-nu-maii, most often, culminated in a bahu mehfil, where the new bride would be called to sing and display her artistic talent and temperament to the in-laws.

It was a ceremony that stressed out many less accomplished brides. It was mandatory to sing, even if it was a few lines

LC gifting jewellery to my mother during the ru-nu-maii, a uniquely Kayasth wedding custom.

out of tune; the elders bestowed an *inaam*, a gift or prize, regardless of how well you sang. Brides-to-be invested much of their time practising a single bhajan or ghazal for this specific occasion, even if they never sang again in their lives. My mother, no singer certainly, bravely did her bit – and kept the fair name of her new family intact. (Considering Mrs LC was such a good singer, every one had expected her to 'choose' a musically inclined daughter-in-law! My mother lived up to the pressure that day.) If refusing to sing was not a choice, refusing the ritualistic peg of whisky was not an option either. My great-grandfather, ecstatic at his eldest grandson getting married, paternalistically and ritualistically proffered a glass of whisky to the new daughter-in-law at the ru-nu-maii. My mother accepted with folded hands, in the customary gesture, sipped a ritualistic sip – and never drank again in her life.

The best Scotch story I've heard concerns a ninety-four-year-old Kayasth matriarch from Gorakhpur, my friend Mahimapat Ray's grandmother, who had a peg of whisky every evening till the day she died. Tara Ray lived well. She was as imperious as Mrs LC, running a household manned by fifteen staff members to do her bidding, having small portions of fish and meat every evening as part of dinner – and drinking four bottles of imported Scotch every month. All part of a routine! If Kayasth men have been deemed shaukeen, evidently, quite a few of the women were too.

Given the spread of the community and the various sub-castes, all seeking to be 'better' than the others, it is inevitable that all Kayasth families are somewhat different from one another even while sharing the same cultural fabric. There are invariably slight variations in customs, in food habits, in economic stature, in how 'liberal' each family is and so on. But there is one overwhelming commonality. And it is in the concept of *khatirdari*, hospitality – making guests feel welcomed. And Kayasth khatirdari revolves around both food and drink. To put it quite simply, it involves not just a lot of non-vegetarian food but also free-flowing whisky (and other liquor). You cannot go to a Kayasth home even today and not be offered substantial amounts of both khana and peena.

Nowhere is this warm-hearted generosity more evident than at a wedding in the family. In more conservative, or perhaps not so well-to-do families, the scale of weddings may be modest. For the Delhi Kayasths, the mehendi meal is important: a set of dishes sent to the groom's family an evening before the main wedding. This is the evening when *henna*, considered auspicious and a symbol of fertility, is put on the bride's and also the groom's hands. Alongside, there is much music and dancing by both the ladies and gentlemen of the two families – separately in their own homes or in a guest accommodation. A relatively modest mehendi meal may feature just one or two non-vegetarian dishes. But at least one bottle of Scotch always accompanies the traditional dishes such as dahi bada, khasta kachori, pickles, chhoti poori and other vegetarian and non-vegetarian items.

In larger, more shaukeen and more moneyed families,

the khana–peena revelry is in a league of its own. When Amrita's brother was getting married to a Kashmiri Pandit girl, her father had just one doubt to clear: do Kashmiri Brahmins eat meat? Reassured on that count, he requested the bride's family to keep enough non-vegetarian fare on the table for the three days that the baraat stayed at their home in Jammu. The marriage procession – about a hundred people, all friends and family – travelling from Kanpur, were booked into a separate railcoupé. A traditional Kayasth caterer was hired for meals on board. And the family carried enough liquor to keep the party going, while travelling and during their stay at the bride's house.

LC, was equally firm about frugal weddings. He strictly forbade my maternal grandfather, Nanaji, Bishan Swaroop, a doctor, from giving any gifts to the family at the time of my parents' wedding. What he requested instead was *poori khatirdari*. Total hospitality. Nanaji, not a gourmet and a man of much moderation in his personal life, followed one philosophy, perhaps from his readings of Osho: let the other person indulge so much that they are totally satiated and don't ask for more. That is how he weaned us out of colas and chocolates and other things he thought of as wasteful or harmful. For the wedding, he ensured so much food and drink for the marriage party that many members were taken ill because of the excess. The good doctor then sent them enough medicines for total recovery! Throughout his life, my nana remained a strict man of few words, deliberate actions, stoic, a vegetarian and a teetotaler. He would use the same pen for years, wear the same shirt and the same perfume, finding shopping a waste of time and money. He read books, practised yoga and got up at 4 a.m. every morning to centre himself with meditation.

In short, his living was quite the opposite of the bacchanalia that pervades many other Kayasth households, and certainly the home of the LCs, the other side of my family. Yet, in the big storeroom of his house in Bareilly, Nanaji kept a locked attaché. It was opened only when my father, the shaukeen son-in-law, came visiting. Inside the suitcase was a bottle of ageing Scotch. Nanaji would offer my father a drink, at least on the first evening he visited. There could be no khatirdari or pampering of the son-in-law without whisky. It is not for nothing that the first gift the son-in-law gets from family elders when he comes to 'take away' his bride (and each time thereafter) is money given in silver bowls. It's called a pyala.

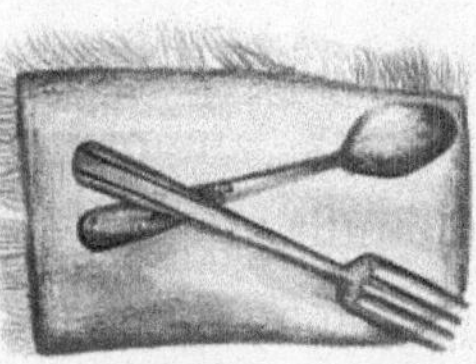

PART III

COLONIALISM AND THE KAYASTH

Kayasth culture and cuisine may have had its genesis in the Indo-Islamic Ganga–Jamuni tehzeeb, but the colonial influence on the community cannot be discounted.

With the disintegration of Mughal power, many Kayasth families were reduced to somewhat dire straits, particularly those in areas of UP and Delhi that continued to be under the rule of the later Mughals. This was unlike areas in Bihar, Bengal, Hyderabad, Rajasthan and the Maratha-ruled parts of northern India where the subsidiary courts had been functioning independently in the absence of a strong emperor in Delhi. The bankrupted treasury could barely pay the salaried Kayasths, affiliated to the courts, or functioning as katibs, mukhtyars and munshis. *Wazifas*, grants and pensions were cancelled, and if Mirza Ghalib, the great poet of Delhi, lived out his last days in poverty, he was hardly alone.

The Kayasths, apparently, held on to their gentility through these years of reduced circumstances. An old community proverb celebrates this sense of self:

Museebat mein bhi Mathuron ki
sharafat kam nahin hoti;

Karo soney ke sau tukde,
magar qeemat kam nahin hoti.

Even in difficult times, the nobility of
the Mathurs remains undiminished;
If you break gold into a hundred small pieces,
its value does not lessen.

Post 1857, as the Company rule ended and India came directly under the Crown, the new empire-building measures began to benefit the literate community both indirectly and directly. India coming under the British crown led to the need for loyal – and educated – aides who understood revenue administration in the districts and towns. The framework of this administrative system had been laid by the great Mughals and records were written in Persian (much of the terminology they used remains till today). The Kayasths were thus invaluable as resources that could help the new powers administer a large, shambolic country like India. The emphasis on education in the community meant that some of the first locals to take up 'English' education were scions of Kayasth families. Gradually, Kayasth fortunes began to rise again.

Once again, a new language became the instrument to gain power and social currency, not to mention material affluence. History seems to have repeated itself also in that the new language of influence became a vehicle for a cultural change within the community itself. The Ganga–Jamuni world of the Kayasths now saw a third influence – 'English'

– which permeated their way of life in myriad ways. Naturally, that led to developments in cuisine. The table became more lavish. Food and hospitality became symbolic of the upward mobility of the new sahibs as they entertained British officialdom, members of the princely states and their social peers. Never ones to shy away from innovation, the Kayasths now made use of newer ingredients brought by the British – everything from green peas to eggs – and cooking techniques, and enhanced their culinary repertoire. The legacy of fusion – of identities and cuisines – continued.

11

The New Bureaucrats

Victorian Mores at the Dining Table

There is a picture, black-and-white naturally, of a time when I must have been about a year and half. My mother and I are eating lunch. Presumably it is my father who is behind the camera. It must have been the three of us on an ordinary day – a small Kayasth family in Jaipur, where my father worked at that time.

The picture is telling in more ways than its grainy black-and-white print suggests. My mother and I are seated at the dining table, a proper meal has been laid out, and even I, all of one and a half, have been given an individual plate and cutlery, a napkin tucked under my chin. 'We were so particular about teaching you then about how to sit at a table and eat properly,' says my mother when we stumble upon the picture.

Regardless of the number of diners or the ordinariness of the occasion, dining at home has never been treated casually in my parents' home. Much of it has to do with the LCs' legacy. The emphasis on a 'complete meal', with at least two vegetables, a dal, roti, rice and condiments on the lunch table, comes down from their time and from generations before. For dinner, and if guests came calling, a meat dish was almost always added to this menu. This was the simplest Kayasth meal, and all homes mostly had similar standards for daily meals. But the emphasis was also on *how* you ate that meal, the *manner* of it. For the LCs, it was the bureaucratic Railways life they led that instilled in them the decorum and manners of minor English aristocrats, at least outwardly.

At Oakgrove, an old boarding school in Jharipani, Mussoorie, LC had a small principal's cottage. The school was established by the British Railways, a private company in the days of the Raj, to cater to the educational needs of the children of officials in the Railways; Indian students too gradually gained admission to the school, as with other schools in the hills. It was a fortuitous appointment for my grandfather because three of his four children were studying in this school set up in sylvan environs, like most boarding schools in India, to emulate the English private schools.

In the evening, the family would congregate in the dining room for dinner. Every member was expected to have changed into formal evening wear, and they would all sit down to their curries and bhuna with a butler in attendance. The table was formally laid. The children were expected to know their cutlery and use it well, and there was an atmosphere of formal quiet in which every meal was eaten. Dining table etiquette was considered to be of paramount importance. Even an early meal like breakfast brooked no deviance. LC was particular that no one came down in their pyjamas or nightclothes. Everyone had to be bathed and properly attired before they could sit down to their parathas and omelettes.

This was much after Independence – in the 1960s – but bureaucratic families like that of the LCs had clung on to notions of Englishness that had seeped into the Kayasth lifestyle at the turn of the twentieth century. This was when educated Kayasths became natural contenders for positions of some prominence opening up to the natives in administration, courts and education – in the civil services under the Crown, in private British companies such as the Railways and the Post and Telegraph services, or in the colleges and universities set up to further an English style of education.

Already an educated community and part of the elite with a major say in administration, the Kayasths were quick to adapt to the new language of power. They seemed to have collectively taken as easily to English and education in English as they had to Persian and Rekhta/Urdu before that. And if they had been an intrinsic part of administration under the Mughals, under the British Crown they began to peddle influence once again.

While many Kayasths found employment in the courts of princely India (as Mrs LC's father had in the court of the Scindias), many other families gravitated to the newly established centres of learning in Rampur and Roorkee, Allahabad, Lucknow and Delhi. The men acquired degrees in engineering or English literature or history or law, and began to teach in the colleges and universities. That is why many Kayasth families today trace their lineage to one of these 'university towns'. When the elite Indian Civil Service was formed in 1858, all its top members were British; by the turn of the century Indians (particularly Kayasths from Bengal) began to make it to the service. Their siblings, children and grandchildren followed in their footsteps, so that entire families came to be known as 'bureaucratic families' – well known and influential in their regions, wielders of power that stemmed from the pen and the seal of governance.

With this, certain elements became part of the Kayasth identity – whisky and bed tea, collections of fine porcelain and women's education in universities, English summer house-style architecture (with the addition of the all-important central courtyard, or *aangan*, of the Indian havelis, around which the rooms of the joint family were spread), distinctive pieces of furniture such as armchairs (the *araamkursis* were a regular feature of affluent Kayasth homes) and fusion dishes such as egg curry, nargisi kofte and makhane matar using the sweet 'English' green pea. And there was the dining table itself, on which these began to be served.

Before the dining table became a fixture in Kayasth homes,

meals would be eaten on individual tables, sometimes in the kitchen, sometimes just outside it, with family members seated on low chowkis, or stools. That was the traditional way of dining. The first 'batch' comprised all the men in the family. Low tables were placed in front of each of them and food was served on thalis made of phool, an alloy. Only the very rich ate out of silver, though in most well-to-do families, water and milk were served in silver glasses. Even at the time that I was growing up, it was common for every child in the family to have her own silver glass with her name inscribed on it.

A maharaj, a Brahmin cook, and his wife presided over the kitchen, making fresh food and serving phulkas straight from the fire to the thalis of the diners. Each maharaj had his retinue of helpers, depending on the economic and social status of the employer's family, and each helper was assigned a task according to his caste and station in life. The maharaj would never deign to cook meat. Even though the Kayasth men were fond of their red meat, eating it almost on a daily basis, traditionally meat was never brought inside the 'pure' inner kitchen that was the domain of the maharaj and the household's womenfolk. In earlier days, meat had to be cooked by one of the 'lower-caste' kitchen hands, in the courtyard, in a separate vessel earmarked for this use.

Gradually, this way of life began to change and become more relaxed as Kayasths adapted to the cultural mores of the new colonial rulers. While some of the Kayasth families were already urban – such as those that lived in Shahjahanabad, invited by Shahjahan himself to take up residence there – others now started moving to the upcoming centres of education, governance and power. They lost their provinciality and became more urbane, at least in their outward lifestyles.

In UP, the erstwhile United Provinces of Oudh and Agra – the original birthplace of the Kayasths – there was a considerable and discernible shift from rural to urban living. Families whose members had been part of the revenue administration in the villages, for instance – patwaris and munshis, keepers of land records – gradually started sending their younger men (and women) to the university towns to experience the British system of education. Often, families with even a single member teaching at a university would host members of the extended clan for years as relatives came to the cities to acquire an education and stay in large, extended joint families.

Women began to be educated in the university system as well, and quite a few, including Mrs LC, not only graduated but earned double bachelor's or master's degrees in different subjects. If they married into families which were regarded as more Westernized, they adopted newer mannerisms. If the Kayasth men, in order to measure up to their British officers or peers, acquired English speech, shirts and suits, and pastimes such as playing tennis at the club or going for 'picnics', the women stuck to their sarees (though the blouse, as we all know, was a Victorian adaptation) but went out ballroom dancing with their husbands or, at the very least, made it their evening ritual to walk up and down the 'promenade' that had come up in the colonial towns. In this they closely imitated the life and style of the upper-class English gentry.

In this world, it was but natural that the dining table and porcelain replace chowki and phool thali within Kayasth homes. The change occurred slowly, in stages. Initially, the dining table was an item of furniture used only for special occasions, installed in an outer 'reception' area of the home where the men of the family in the service of the British could entertain other officers and colleagues. Close family members and the women would still eat in the kitchen or the courtyard at their low tables. However, over time, the older way of life gave way to the new. By the time the LCs were married, the dining table stood for much more than its utilitarian aspect; it had become a metaphor. For these privileged Kayasths who had found power through proximity with the rulers, the dining table was a symbol of sophistication, urbanization and upward mobility that set them apart in their way of life from other Indian families. It defined their new status as 'progressive' and 'enlightened' Indians, at ease in the world of the colonial sahibs, sharing their values and lifestyle, being the quintessential brown sahibs. Inevitably, there was much attention and emphasis on not just what was laid out on the table, but *how* it was done.

LC was still in service and at the height of his power bestowed by the Government of India when I went to stay with my grandparents in Banaras as a three-year-old and imbibed some of that imperiousness that comes from being raised in a family of bureaucrats with privilege and as an only child in a house full of doting adults. Everyone – from my grandmother to the cook, to the gardener and the general errands-person – was there to do my bidding. Or so I thought, as a tiny tot. When I came back from pre-school, I expected the lunch table to be set and laid out 'properly' for me. There needed to be a glass of freshly squeezed orange juice or sweet lime juice waiting and the cook had instructions to make egg curry, my favourite dish, for lunch every day. Or bhindi the other favourite I would never tire of. This was part of an unchanging daily ritual. After the meal, off I went for an afternoon siesta, Barima telling me stories till I dozed off.

On some days, however, despite my insistence on table mats and cutlery and full plates, I would be bored and wish to experience other ways of eating, other foods. Such as that of our cook, Vidur. In my long conversations with him, I had heard of this wonderful dish, denied to me but eaten every day in his home in the outhouse of the LCs' huge bungalow – 'dal–bhaat'. It became to me the most wondrous, mysterious dish on the planet. Arhar dal was a regular on our table. But what was this thing called 'bhaat', I wondered; would I never get a chance to sample it? Every day, I would try to persuade Barima to allow me to eat with Vidur and Malti, his wife, and their kids in their home. I had also heard of the way they ate; the ritual of eating seated on a low *patra*, a thin wooden plank or stool, with the thali placed on the floor, seemed unutterably exotic to me. Every day, Barima would deny me permission. Then one day, probably fed up with my incessant whining, she asked Vidur and his children to cook and eat their meal in our kitchen. Finally, I was invited to eat the way they did. Not at the dining table.

We sat down on the floor, thalis placed in front of us, on which the yellow pigeon pea typical of eastern UP and some fragrant rice were served. I can't remember if there was anything else to supplement the meal. There may have been some vegetable plucked fresh from the garden on the premises. All I can recall is the sharp taste of disappointment. That mysterious, fascinating, delicious-sounding dal–bhaat had turned out to be a most ordinary dish. My childish brain could not reconcile the exotic sound of bhaat with the familiar, boring chawal, or plain boiled rice. For days after that I was convinced it was a sleight of hand on the part of the adults to cheat me out of eating a wonderful new dish! Dal–bhaat on a patra was as commonplace as dal–chawal at the dining table: there was a lesson here far beyond the scope of my comprehension of childish mind.

12

The Language of Power

How the Kayasths Switched Sides

If language was the cultural tool that Kayasths used to thrive in new orders, seeking education first in Persian, then Rekhta/Urdu and then English, it naturally also became a marker of their more 'elite' way of life. The old Kayasth families of Shahjahanabad, Agra and Lucknow, whose members were associated with the Mughal courts, had become urbanized fairly early. Many others, whose members had functioned in villages and districts as part of the land revenue administrative system under the Mughals, became gradually urbanized with the coming of the British. The urban families had a distinct way of speaking. While Kayasths under the British studied English as an 'official' language of sorts, using it for work, studying its literature, and even referring to it in their day-to-day lives – as LC was wont to, peppering his talks with lines from Shakespeare, Shelley or Milton – the language used at home was a fairly refined version of Hindustani, quite distinct in its liberal use of Urdu words, their correct and clear pronunciation insisted upon. Any of us who pronounced a word wrong would be pulled up and branded 'uncultured'. The words showed the family/community's urbanization quite clearly. Instead of 'bhaat', the word for boiled rice in Maithili or Bhojpuri or Avadhi, our mother tongue, the language of our ancestors, we used 'chawal', the more urbanized word for rice, so much so that, as I have just recounted, as a child I mistook 'bhaat' to be the name of an altogether different, exotic dish.

My grandparents' everyday speech was sprinkled with words that you don't hear any more – unless, of course, you are speaking to someone from an old Kayasth or Muslim family from UP. Words like *niyamat* (a rare gift or divine blessing), usually used by the LCs to describe some sublime food, *qayamat* (end of the world), usually referring to a mock crisis in the household, *hazm* (digest) and *nazm* (poetry) were all used in their day-to-day speech.

Consonants like 'g', 'kh' and 'k' in Hindi were pronounced in their Urdu way as 'gh', 'x' and 'q' – 'gharib', instead of 'garib' in Hindi; 'xud', the guttural sound, instead of 'khud' in Hindi, and 'qalam', instead of 'kalam'. Similarly, 'v' or 'w' after a long vowel was always rounded off to 'o' in the Urdu way of speaking. We said 'pulao' instead of 'pulav', 'tanaao' instead of 'tanav'. And 'w' became silent in 'khwaab'; it was simply 'khaab' – so much more poetic. There were many more common words that we used, unthinkingly, following the Urdu pronunciation rather than the *shudh* Hindi one being taught in schools, used in the bookish phrases propagated in the newsrooms and offices in Independent India, and enunciated by TV newsreaders.

The element that definitively marked out a rustic style of speech from a refined one in the minds of my grandparents (and hence mine) was the 'z'/'j' barrier. In UP, non-Kayasth families from more rural backgrounds would say 'subji' (not 'subzi', which was the Urdu pronunciation), 'jeera' (not 'zeera') and 'jameen' (not 'zameen'), and such speech was deeply scorned by the LCs. Growing up in their company, I was equally disdainful. This difference in the way my grandparents (and we) spoke and the way the rest of the Hindi heartland spoke led to a fair bit of skirmishes and linguistic rivalry when I went to school, as friends from different backgrounds used different pronunciations.

As courtiers to the Mughal kings and wielders of influence in British India, the educated Kayasths understood, like no one else perhaps, how language could be the key to power. It was their early adaptation of Persian, the court language, which had after all been responsible for the rise in their fortunes.

As the original language of synthesis between Persian, Avadhi and Khari Boli, Rekhta or Urdu was not just the language of the upper-class Muslims of the Indo-Gangetic plains but of all those who shared in the power of the great and later-day minor Mughals. It came naturally to the Kayasths, at the epicentre of this world of fusion, who spoke Rekhta/Urdu as well as their local dialect of Hindi. And it remained with them long after the power had shifted, first to the British crown and later to the nationalists who fought and won the country its freedom, their narrative propelling Hindi as the 'national' language of a linguistically disparate country. With each shift in power, the Kayasths adapted, absorbing first English education and acquiring great felicity in the Victorian version of the language, and then quickly learning the Hindi of a newly independent, resilient India.

This is brought home forcefully to me as I chat one summer afternoon in Noida with veteran bureaucrat Prabhas Kumar, formerly a member of the Cabinet Secretariat and an ex-governor of Jharkhand. Sitting in an armchair, surrounded by books, Mr Kumar reminds me of LC in many ways. Perhaps it is his way of speaking, his speech dotted with Urdu words, the diction immaculate. Perhaps it is his erudition and the enthusiastic manner in which he shows me an original lithograph of the Constitution of India, or perhaps it is the manner in which he quizzes me.

'Do you know that only 500 lithographic prints were made of the Constitution? And that it has sketches by Nandalal Bose and calligraphy by Prem Behari Narain Raizada, both Kayasths?' Mr Kumar asks, before hastening to his library to fetch me a prized copy of the Constitution, one of the 500 initially produced. While I knew about the Nandalal Bose illustrations, I did not know that it was a Saxena from an old Delhi family who had in fact calligraphed the Constitution.

Mr Kumar, rightly takes a great deal of pride and pleasure in the community's erudition as LC would have.

It is to perhaps check my level of learning that he gently quizzes me: 'My father's name was Oudh Behari Lall, spelled the British way. Oudh Behari – do you know what that means?'

Caught by surprise, I nod. 'Of course, a resident of Avadh,' I say, literally translating the term 'Oudh Behari'.

'Arrey, Ram Chandraji!' he exclaims, referring to the mythic god, who in his human avatar ruled Avadh (Ayodhya) and is thus referred to as Avadh Bihari in much of literature and folklore. Avadh Bihari Ram is the family deity for many Kayasth families, including mine.

The slight glee with which the question has been posed to me reminds me of LC's favourite poser to his English-speaking students at Oakgrove: 'What language is the *Ramcharitmanas* written in?' A surprising number of people apparently failed this test, mumbling 'Sanskrit', upon which my grandfather would triumphantly proclaim: 'Avadhi.' It was a story narrated to us so many times that I have a vivid mental picture of LC educating the clueless students on a bit of 'our culture' – and language.

This preoccupation with language has to be a Kayasth trait, I decide. The impression is reinforced when Mr Kumar tells me his family's story and its tryst with a dramatic switch of languages. Born into a landed family from Etawah, both Oudh Behari Lall and his brother studied at the Thompson College in Roorkee (now the Indian Institute of

Technology there). The style they adopted for their names and surname is perhaps a fair indicator of the family's quick adaptation of Englishness. While Oudh Behari Lall joined the Post and Telegraph services, his brother joined the Railways, both private companies in British India with a predominantly British staff. Oudh Behari was posted in Allahabad. He became one of the few Indian officers in town and maintained close ties with other British officers, entertaining them at home, playing tennis with them in the club, walking along the 'mall' with his wife and even taking her ballroom dancing.

'We were a highly anglicized family,' says Mr Kumar. 'My elder brothers and sisters and I were all educated in English-medium missionary schools.' But at the stroke of midnight, on 15 August 1947, as the British left India and the country became free, they 'were taken out of English-medium schools and put into Hindi-medium schools... Right on that day. On 15 August 1947...' he trails off. It is an astounding statement. As I listen to the family tales and think of the Kayasth lifestyle as reflected in these stories, I can't help but turn these words over and over again in my mind: 'Right on that day. On 15 August 1947...'

Was it merely a symbolic gesture made out of a sense of patriotism sweeping the country, and Allahabad most certainly, at that point in our history? The town was a hotbed of political activity. The Lalls had known many of the Allahabad-based Congress leaders closely enough; Lal Bahadur Shastri (another Kayasth) was a neighbour and called Mr Lall's wife his sister. There were many others who were known to the family and whose views on freedom the Lalls were sympathetic to, even though they benefitted from the British Raj and did not give up any of those privileges. Or, was it also, at some level, the call of an inherited trait of adaptibility to change, of taking on another new language as a cultural tool for survival that prompted this decision? It could have been either. Or, most likely, both.

13

The New Colonial Dishes

And How Kayasth Men Entered the Kitchen

One of the behaviour patterns of the community that fascinates people is why many Kayasth men cook so well. This is quite exceptional in the larger Indian society, which is highly patriarchal, with specific gender roles firmly in place. '*Maa ke haath ka khana*', a mother's cooking, revered across the subcontinent may be a legend at par with the mythic Italian mama's cooking but in many Kayasth households the father's cooking is equally venerated and looked up to.

My father is an exceptional cook, the flavours of his kofte (made of keema, naturally), pasande and bhuna meat having found fame within the family and among his circle of friends. In the home of the LCs, however, LC was hardly the cook. He was more of a culinary director, appreciating new flavours, encouraging others to cook and experiment, but also sharply critical of botched gourmet attempts. I know of many other Kayasth men who are more directly involved in exercising their passion for fine food, and it may be interesting to conjecture how this trait developed in the community.

While Kayasth men do cook, they predominantly cook meat. Shikaar, or hunting, seems to have been the prime facilitator of this passion for cooking.

With the disintegration of the Mughal empire and the onset of British rule, much of it through proxy governments in the princely states, many of the educated Kayasths, well versed in administration, revenue administration and services such as engineering, sought employment in the courts of principalities such as Gwalior, Jaipur, Bhopal, Patiala, Hyderabad, Rampur and other minor states. Elaborate shikaars, or royal hunts, were part of the entertainment of this princely life, in which both the royals and young British officers participated.

As part of the feudal courts, Kayasth men inevitably participated in these hunts, socializing with both the royals and the British officers. In other, more rural parts of eastern UP, Bihar and Bengal, Kayasths loyal to the British administration were awarded the titles of Rai Zada or Rai Bahadur and gifted land; they functioned as zamindars, collecting 'rent' from farmers who cultivated their land, contributing to the upkeep of the British treasury and armed forces, and hosting lavish entertainment for the officers, including hunts, poetry, music and dance sessions, and grand dinners. Such entertainment contributed not only to the development of Kayasth cuisine but also of the larger lifestyle in which both poetry and the arts took centre stage.

In this regard, the Rai-Ray family from Gorakhpur makes for an interesting study. Erstwhile zamindars of Rai Ramgarh Tal, a huge lake located in Gorakhpur district in UP, the Rai-Ray family traces its history to Rai Bahoran Das, who lived 175 years ago. A Srivastava from Allahabad, Rai Bahoran Das came to this region of eastern UP with the Mughal army. The title 'Rai' was bestowed on him by the Mughals, and he became one of the three zamindars of this Terai region, based in a village named after the family, Rai Sahrari.

When the British overthrew the Mughals and banished the last Nawab of Avadh, Wajid Ali Shah, to Bengal, the Rai family turned to the new rulers, feeding their army and earning a new title, 'Ray', the anglicized form of 'Rai' shortened from Rai Bahadur. Rai Mahipat Ray, with the double-barrel Rai-Ray prefix and suffix, and his brother Rai Sabhapati Ray became, respectively, the chairman of the municipality and the general manager of the sugar mill in Gorakhpur. Between themselves they inherited the contract for fisheries in two huge lakes (though one is now disputed) and a *hatha*, or compound, of 60 acres, including a 150-year-old Shiv temple.

Today, their descendants, six brothers, have separate houses in the same compound, which they share with around twenty-five tenants. Their feudal lifestyle is well on the wane, a pale reflection of what it once was. Nutan

Ray, one of the owners, tells me of the old days when her father-in-law, the grand patriarch, still lived like a zamindar. 'Every new bride in the family was first taken out boating in the lake and the fishermen who worked for us cooked a meal by the edge of water with the day's catch. It was a sort of picnic,' she recalls. Then there were the hunts. Venison kebabs were the family's speciality. Small birds – 'like bater [quail] and bagheri [a kind of lark]' – were bhunoed in lots of onion and garlic 'to take away the smell', she says.

While a Brahmin cook supervised the main kitchen, game – as also meat and fish – was not cooked there. In the army of staff employed to run the huge household, there were people from different castes and religions, and strict roles were assigned to each. For instance, the tailors and the *miskar*, or washerwomen, were either 'lower-caste' or Muslim, says Ray, as were the *baheliya*, traditionally bird hunters. These were the people who looked after poultry; often, it was the baheliya who were called upon to clean and cook game after a hunt.

Some Kayasth women may have eventually learned to excel at cooking venison kofte and kebabs, teetar (partridge) and bater, as also raan, but most of them remained vegetarian; in many families it was the men who took to cooking game and other meats on a weekly basis in the outer, separate kitchens with help from the staff, who were Muslim or from a 'lower caste'. That Kayasth men now have almost a genetic disposition to cooking, especially meat, can perhaps be seen as an internalization of this early lifestyle.

Kayasth cuisine, highly influenced by the Mughals, has a rich repertoire of red meat dishes, but chicken was not part of the community's traditional culinary repertoire. The bird was not popular in medieval India though certain recipes using it were part of the Mughal repertoire. Meat-eating, 'upper-caste', upper-class Hindu communities like the Kayasths considered it 'unclean' because the fowl was considered a scavenger. It was a belief that perhaps gradually spread to Muslims in the Indo-Gangetic plain, who also preferred red meat. Poultry as an industry developed largely in British India. As a result, eggs gradually became popular, even with fairly traditional Indian communities. But chicken still didn't quite make the cut – even with the Kayasths. It would take several more years and a bloody Partition for the fowl to become northern India's most preffered bird to eat, and many more years before the cheeky innovation of 'chicken biryani' became acceptable in Kayasth homes. The pulao, on the other hand, thankfully remained sacrosanct, and continued to be made only from goat meat.

With the entry of eggs into the daily lives of the Kayasth brown sahibs, the breakfast table began to look different. So far, breakfast had been dominated by such dishes as wholesome paratha–subzi or chhoti namkeen pooris flavoured with ajwain. It was really a brunch, a rare morning meal that people ate. These pooris took the form of nagori halwa in Delhi, where they were filled with hot semolina halwa on winter mornings. But now omelettes, boiled eggs and 'crisp' fried eggs, generously seasoned with salt and pepper, found an assured place on the dining table along with 'double roti', or sliced bread. The Kayasth women who refused to eat eggs found an alternative to these breakfasts. Mrs LC was one of these women and sometimes took great pleasure in breakfasting on 'naqli omelette' – a pancake made with bread and besan.

Eggs became the basis of two great innovations that became very popular in Kayasth homes during the colonial period: egg curry and nargisi kofta. The former is a dish of boiled eggs fried till reddish-brown and then curried in a rich, well-bhunoed gravy of onion–garlic–ginger. Nargisi kofta is a spin on the keema kofta, with a hard-boiled egg placed in the centre of a round of mince, which is then curried. Like many dishes invented during that time in upper-class homes that interacted with the British and had access to the best of ingredients, it is impossible to say whether the egg curry and the nargisi kofta are 'Kayasth' dishes. It is fair to assume that with the fall from power of the Muslim elite, it was the well-to-do Kayasth families, fond of eating Mughal-style meat dishes, who patronized old Muslim cooks in cities such as Delhi, Lucknow and Calcutta. Many of the 'new' dishes that originated in this period of cultural confluence came about as a result of this patronage. Dishes like shabdeg, popular with the Delhi Kayasths but never made at home, only commissioned for feasts, nargisi kofta and even dum aloo are some of them. To prepare dum aloo, using the old Muslim technique of dum was used to cook new, small potatoes of the season, extensively cultivated by the British after their introduction into India by Dutch traders. They are the typical feast or party dishes in many Kayasth homes even today.

Chef Ghulam Qureshi of Dum Pukht, the renowned Avadhi specialty restaurant at ITC Maurya, New Delhi, reminds me of the close connection shared by affluent Kayasth homes with Muslim cooks across the Indo-Gangetic plain as well as in places such as Hyderabad, a city that also has a substantial Kayasth presence thanks to the migration of the community to the Nizam's court. The Qureshi surname is highly respected in the restaurant business. Chef Ghulam is the nephew and son-in-law of the Padma Shri awardee Chef Imtiaz Qureshi, whose legendary talent has been instrumental in popularizing the Avadhi style of dum cooking across the country and even internationally. A family of butchers from Lucknow, they trace their lineage back 200 years to the Nawabi days, when assorted members worked in various capacities for the 'rajas' of Avadh. The family eventually turned to catering, with Chef Imtiaz Qureshi cooking at Krishna Hotel and Clarks, both popular in Lucknow till as late as the 1980s – and catching the eye of Pandit Jawaharlal Nehru India's first Prime Minister, as the story goes.

How the Qureshis moved from Lucknow to five-star cooking in Delhi and how, from Dum Pukht in ITC Maurya, family members spread to various hotel and restaurant kitchens, defining the way in which much of Indian 'Mughlai' cuisine is commercially served today, is a fascinating account in its own right. But each time I meet Chef Ghulam Qureshi, he remembers the good old days in Lucknow, when he had apprenticed with Chef Imtiaz Qureshi, catered to my alma mater La Martinere and cooked for the families of the predominantly Kayasth neighbourhood in Lucknow, Ghasiyari Mandi. 'They were the patrons who knew their food,' says the chef, not infrequently, of those 'good old days'.

In Daryaganj, Delhi, Mrs Rajesh Dayal, owner of one of the last single-owner Kayasth havelis in that part of town, remembers the 'good old days' as well. The haveli stands as an oasis of quiet in the crowded and commercial lanes of Daryaganj, the last of the colonial-style homes built by the Kayasths here, on the banks of the Yamuna. 'As a child in the 1930s, I played in the foundations of this house,' says Mrs Dayal. The Terrace, as the haveli is called, is a British-style duplex, built by Dayal's father-in-law, a civil engineer employed in the court of Kota. It was completed in 1935 and its architecture and design elements – the *roshandan*s or skylights (six in each room), fireplaces and coloured stone floor (neither marble nor tiled but with patterns that remind you of Shyam Ahuja's exquisitely woven carpets) stand testimony to the elegance of the years gone by.

Mrs Dayal sits in an araamkursi in the veranda, which overlooks a slightly overgrown garden. This is the house's central courtyard into which each of the rooms opens. You can still hear the birds chirp and feel the gentle evening breeze in summer, when everything outside is unbearably hot and chaotic. It's the perfect spot to reminisce, and Rajesh Dayal, well into her eighties now, does just that.

With many joint Kayasth families living in the same neighbourhood, the children of the *biradri*, or fraternity, were closely bonded, their lives punctuated by common celebrations: festivals, weddings and large community gatherings that called for huge feasts. Muslim cooks patronized by the families would be called from Ballimaran and Motia Mahal in the Jama Masjid area, just across the road, to cook their specialities. 'There was this cook called Booby,' Dayal remembers, 'who made the best shabdeg ever. My mouth waters even now at its memory...' To cook shabdeg, the meat-and-turnip winter special of old Delhi, a Muslim cook favoured by the Kayasth family in question would build an old style earthen oven on an empty patch of land near the mansion. A pit would be dug and a sealed pot of meat, spices and turnips placed over smouldering embers; this would then be covered and some more live coals placed on top. The meat stewed slowly the entire night and was served as a winter lunch the next day.

There are other similar dishes that seem to have crept into the community's repertoire across India. In Bengal, it is almost impossible to differentiate 'Kayasth' cooking from 'upper-caste' Hindu cooking ('upper-caste' Hindus also eat meat and fish in that state). Many of the dishes don't just bear a distinct colonial imprint but are part of a legacy created by Kayasth–Brahmin landlords hiring old Muslim cooks for banquets in which they entertained

British officers. Many of the dishes – from kosha mangsho (Bengali mutton curry) to raw jackfruit cooked on dum – are therefore reminiscent of the Kayasth cooking of UP. If Bengal has meat chaap, mochar chop, or banana flower cutlets, and aloo dum, the UP and Delhi Kayasths have chaap/chops (always made from goat meat), as also potato chop (a popular evening snack in Kayasth homes) and dum aloo. In Delhi the potato chop would be stuffed with chana dal, in UP with fresh green peas. Both are colonial legacies designed after the cutlet.

The new colonial dishes changed from region to region with minor tweaking of ingredients and spices. For instance, there is a difference in the spices used in the UP-style dum aloo of my family and the aloo dum of Bengali homes. Both badi elaichi (the nutty-smelling black cardamom) and black peppercorns went into the dum aloo on Mrs LC's table. The potatoes were fried until reddish brown, the souring agent was whisked yoghurt, and the curry was kept thick. The Bengali aloo dum recipe that I got from a friend uses heeng with the onion masala (a no-no in my home), a pinch of sugar and bay leaves along with other spices. The potatoes are not deep-fried but sautéed in the masala, and the final dish is drier than the UP version. Both are typically slow-cooked on dum, and not in the pressure cooker, which is how families may cook them today. While in the home of the LCs we would eat the dish with poori, in Bengali homes luchi is the right bread to scoop these up with. Minor differences; the same dish.

Often cooks also used newer ingredients popular with the Europeans to create more exotic versions of older dishes. These included vegetables such as green pea and potato, which we think of as fairly commonplace today but which were regarded as more exotic than, say, seasonal greens and colocasia, the starch of choice in UP till the potato usurped its position. Mince kofte stuffed with fresh green peas or indeed just keema matar and keema mirch (mince cooked with fresh green peas and green chillies respectively), murgh and mahi mussalam (whole chicken and fish) and even gobhi mussalam (whole cauliflower), as also chaap (chop), all seem to be innovations from the days of the Raj. Even till the late 1980s and early 90s, various Kayasth gatherings, weddings and cultural gatherings saw these traditional cooks – whose families had been patronized by affluent Kayasth families for generations – being summoned to cook the specials. My father finally learned his recipe for badam pasanda not from the family specialist, his aunt Mrs KC, but from the cook who came for our annual Mathur sabhas post Diwali. Even when the Kayasths of old Delhi had shifted out to specific localities in east and south Delhi and elsewhere, with many related families taking up flats in adjoining areas, weddings or Holi and Diwali functions would see cooks from the old city wielding their ladles. Sadly, few of them survive today. Their children and apprentices in the catering business too seem to have forgotten the old recipes and are more likely to offer butter chicken than nargisi kofta when planning a menu.

The nargisi kofta and the egg curry, popular Kayasth 'party' dishes, however, survive in homes. Both are specials of my family – the egg curry in particular. Like the nargisi kofta, the egg curry too is a dish that seems to have existed in nineteenth- and early twentieth-century Britain, as an example of early 'fusion'. If the nargisi kofta is indeed the original version of the original Scotch eggs (or vice versa), egg curry shows up as 'Eggs, Curried' in *Cassell's Dictionary of Cookery* of the 1870s, the earliest written reference to this genre of dish.

The English recipe is as follows:

- Fry a couple of medium-sized onions in butter and stir one tablespoonful of curry powder into the pan, as soon as the onions are slightly browned. Mix well.
- Add by degrees half a pint of veal stock.
- Keep stirring the sauce till it is smooth and thick.
- When the mixture has simmered for 10–15 minutes, add 2 tbsp cream, stirring constantly and carefully.
- Let it simmer a few minutes longer.
- Have ready half a dozen hard boiled eggs, sliced in half.
- Lay them in the curry sauce long enough for them to absorb the heat well.
- Then serve both together on a dish.

Not quite the Kayasth egg curry, but close enough!

14

Regional Cook-offs

Local Influences on Kayasth Food

The spread of Kayasth families to different parts of the country gained momentum with the arrival of the British. The rise of British imperialism presented new employment opportunities and small-town families from UP gradually made a shift eastwards. This dispersal affected the Ganga–Jamuni cuisine of Kayasths. Always inventive, Kayasth cooks now began making use of local ingredients, adapting their cuisine to the region in which they settled.

Kayasth cuisine was already evolving at this time because of the availability of newer ingredients brought in by the Europeans. The Dutch had introduced potatoes to the subcontinent. Slowly, as cultivation increased, this vegetable replaced earlier ingredients, such as arvi, that had traditionally gone into the kaliya of UP homes as a starchy supplement to the meat in the curry. Even today, while aloo-meat curry may be more popular, there are older recipes for arvi-meat curry – a traditional combo of fried pieces of colocasia and meat in a curry.

But regional influences offered additional spins to older recipes, as we have seen. It may be an interesting exercise to compare Kayasth dishes of Delhi, UP, Bihar/eastern UP and Bengal, including the food that is part of the generic Bengali repertoire. The same dish appears under different names and with slight variations. The 'do pyaaza' of some families in eastern UP, for instance – where onions are cut into rings and meat is layered between two layers of these onions (along with garlic, ghee and whole garam masala) and left to cook on dum in a sealed kadhai, till tender – reminds me of old Delhi's most popular Mathur-Kayasth dish, khade masale ka bhuna gosht (meat cooked in whole spices).

The dish, whose recipe seems to be standard across most families that trace their lineage to Shahar, is similar to that of the old Delhi Mughlai dish we know as the 'ishtoo'. A colonial dish referencing the 'stew', this is a dish in which onions, meat and whole spices are left to stew in their own juices, on slow fire, till the meat is tender. The most famous and delicious old Delhi ishtoo is the 'dry' one, without any gravy. The Kayasth khade masale ka bhuna gosht is the same, which is also the same as the do pyaaza, with just an extra layer of onions added, no doubt a touch of Nawabi refinement.

Then there are the more ancient dishes – such as alan ka saag, a unique dish of the old Delhi Mathurs – which is essentially an improvization of the UP moong dal-palak recipe that could be found on Mrs LC's table. A little besan beaten into curd (as for kadhi) is added to the well-cooked, mashed chilka moong dal and spinach to give it a smoother consistency and richness. The Dilli-wallas also cook their bharwan karela in a slightly different way from the UP-wallas. The latter pride themselves on their sophistication of combining browned onions with a masala of amchoor and fennel, stuffing this into the karela, tying it with a string and browning it. Delhi's 'chaat papdi' innovativeness – the tendency to use more dahi and imli (yoghurt and tamarind) – sees old families cook 'shorve wale karela' in a gravy, using tamarind water instead of amchoor for sourness.

Usha Kishore Baghwala, from Agra, remembers the cooking of her paternal home in Delhi as less 'bhuna hua', less rich, than the cooking at her in-laws' home in Agra. The khana of the Dilli-wallas was considered lighter, with less use of oil and ghee, and perhaps the addition of more yoghurt, than the rich food of the Agra and Lucknow families. The Baghwalas, who got their family name and lands from the mango orchards given to them by the British, shifted into a 200-year-old home in Agra's Peepal Mandi, earlier owned by a Muslim family but bought over by the newly influential Kayasths. Even today, despite the fact that most Kayasth families have shifted out of the old area and the abolition of zamindari that took away all their lands, Baghwala House stands as the custodian of its past, its forty rooms inhabited by a joint family that takes turns to stay on the premises and look after their home and a temple in the vicinity.

'When I got married, my mother-in-law taught me all

there is to know about cooking,' says Mrs Baghwala, a versatile home cook. Many of the Baghwala recipes comprise different takes on common Kayasth dishes. Not only do they cook the badam pasande of Delhi in the original and dexterous Kayasth way – stuffed (with onions, green chillies and dried fruit) and rolled up – they also specialize in a dish called pateele ke pasande, in which flat pieces of meat are layered with whole spices, nuts and onions, and cooked on dum, with yoghurt added as the souring agent.

The proximity of Peepal Mandi to Bundelkhand, a large part of which is in MP, also means some regional innovations in snacks. Instead of the moong dal ki pakori of Delhi and UP, eaten as a fritter or lightly curried (as favoured by Barima), the favourite snack during the monsoon in the Baghwala home is a pakori made with uneven pieces of boiled potatoes and onions, with roughly pounded coriander seeds as the spice. Barima, who had grown up in Gwalior, had contributed the mangore to my grandfather's UP family repertoire and this became the standard snack in the home of the LCs. When Mrs Baghwala told me about the recipe for her own aloo-bhari pakori, I realized it was mangore by another name. Gwalior and Agra are not that far apart in distance and taste, it appears.

A dish that is so representative of Kayasth cooking that it cuts across divides of regions and sub-castes and is made in virtually every Kayasth home is the yakhni pulao – the Holy Grail of Kayasth khana. It is a quintessential home dish: no fancy or 'exotic' ingredients or masalas are used, the subtlety of the pulao relying entirely on the quality of old, full-grain Basmati rice, the cuts of meat, the careful judgement as to the ratio of stock to rice, as also the length of time required to cook both the rice and meat together and perfectly. There is very little variation in the way this dish is cooked in different Kayasth sub-castes; at the most there are minor divergences, such as Chef Manu Chandra's family recipe, as we have seen, laying more stress on fennel than Mrs LC's does.

Yakhni pulao calls for good quality Basmati rice. However, the rice, highly favoured by UP and Delhi Kayasths, seems to lose its sheen as one moves east. In the Ray home in Gorakhpur, for instance, the rice of choice is the short-grained, sticky Kanak Jeer or Sugandha, eaten with different types of birds and fish of the Terai region. Chidiya–bhaat, literally bird–rice, was the special-occasion feast of the Kayasth landlords who enjoyed game. Bater and bagheri were cooked in onion and garlic in the trademark bhuna Kayasth method, so that the smell of the meat disappeared. This was a dish with very little gravy, paired with the small-grained rice of the region. If most of the UP Kayasths ate kaleji, or liver, again bhunoed in masala, the Terai Kayasths also ate fried fish belly from the rohu or other big fish caught in their lakes. In fact, rohu, typically associated with Bengali food, was traditionally cooked in these Kayasth homes with a *thanda*, cold, masala of mustard, garlic, haldi and fenugreek seeds, again reminiscent of Bengali cooking.

However, nothing is more startling than the journey of the dhokha, literally 'falsehood', as it travels from western and central UP to its eastern fringes and further on. We have discussed one of the things that Mrs LC, the Vaishnavite vegetarian that she was, liked to both cook and eat: the faux liver preparation kaleji ki subzi, or moong dal paste shaped into nuggets, with the masala and texture mimicking a bhuna liver preparation. In Agra, Mrs Baghwala taught me a similar recipe. Hers uses deseeded jamun fruit, ground to a paste, to colour the faux liver before the lentil dumplings are fried. These are then stir-fried in a dry masala, the way many Kayasth homes cook real liver, and eaten as snack, not as a curry. Almost the same recipe is replicated in the Ray home in Gorakhpur, where Nutan Ray uses besan, mixes it into a dough with a seasoning of onions and green chillies, makes a big laddoo of this, steams it in water, then quarters the flour, and fries the pieces till crisp, before dunking them either in shorva (curry) for dinner or eating them dry, as a breakfast dish. But instead of 'kaleji', the dish here, in the home of the Terai Srivastavas, is called 'dhokha'.

Is the dhokar dalna of Bengal a continuation of the same link? Made with yet another lentil – chana dal, Bengal gram – which is local, this dish uses the same methods of cooking, and to the same end: to masquerade taste, to present it as something that it is not. Paheli ka khana, a falsehood served up yet another way. The creative Kayasths would certainly have approved.

Recipes

Egg Curry

A favourite in the home of the LCs, this dish was my obsession through childhood, along with bhindi.

Serves 4

INGREDIENTS

- 4 eggs
- 4 potatoes, the size of eggs, peeled, scored with a knife and deep-fried till reddish brown
- 4 tbsp oil and oil for frying
- 1 tbsp ginger paste
- 1 tbsp garlic paste
- 500g onion paste
- 1 black cardamom, pounded to lightly crack the shell
- Salt to taste
- 100g tomato purée
- ½ tsp turmeric powder
- 1 tsp red chilli powder
- 1 tsp coriander powder
- 2–3 cups of water
- 1 tsp garam masala powder
- A small bunch of fresh green coriander, finely chopped

METHOD

Boil the eggs and deep-fry till golden brown.

Use the same oil to deep-fry the potatoes.

In a heavy-bottomed pan, heat oil and sauté the ginger and garlic pastes.

Then add the onion paste and salt and sauté it till the masala turns reddish brown. Add the black cardamom and stir fry for 1 minute till it releases its aroma.

Now add the tomato purée and the dry spices other than the garam masala. Sauté some more till the oil floats on top.

Add the eggs and potatoes, and the water. Cover and cook on dum, on a low flame, till the potatoes are well done. Adjust the water if necessary to get a thick gravy. If you add water make sure to bring the curry to a boil.

Sprinkle with the garam masala powder and chopped coriander leaves.

Dum ka Kathal

My great-grandfather, who had turned vegetarian in his later years, loved jackfruit, which when cooked right approximated the texture and taste of meat. The trick to cooking kathal well is in choosing the right fruit – it needs to be very tender and without seeds, the kathli, as UP families call it. You could curry it after bhuno-ing in yoghurt, or you could cook it on dum as in this recipe, spiced with badi elaichi, or black cardamom, which has a slightly nutty aroma and is an important spice used in cooking in UP and Delhi.

Serves 4

INGREDIENTS

2 cups oil

Garam masala

- 3 black cardamom, pounded
- 3–4 bay leaves
- 3–4 cinnamon sticks
- 8–10 cloves

1kg raw jackfruit, skin removed and cut into small cubes

1kg onions, sliced

½ tsp turmeric powder

2 tsp coriander powder

2 tsp red chilli powder

1 cup yoghurt, whisked

Salt to taste

METHOD

In a kadhai, heat the oil and add the garam masala.

Once the aroma is released, add the jackfruit cubes and sauté it till they are reddish brown.

Now add the sliced onions and gently bhuno both the onions and kathal on a low flame for 5 minutes.

Add the dry masalas and salt, and stir in the yoghurt. Bhuno for an additional 5–7 minutes.

Cover and cook till well done. Then uncover and bhuno again for about 5–7 minutes.

Serve with rotis.

Mangore

A regional special from Bundelkhand and Gwalior, mangore are fritters flavoured with roughly pounded coriander seeds. The mangore has a rougher, uneven shape than the round pakoris. Ideally served with Scotch!

Serves 4

INGREDIENTS

1kg moong dhuli, soaked and coarsely ground
3 large onions, chopped
4 large potatoes, boiled and roughly chopped
4 green chillies, finely chopped
2 tbsp green coriander leaves, finely chopped
3 tbsp whole coriander seeds, roughly pounded
Salt to taste
Oil for frying

METHOD

Make a batter with the dal and all the other ingredients.

Heat enough oil in a kadhai to deep fry the fritters. When it is smoking hot, scoop little dollops of the batter with your hand, and drop one by one into the oil. Deep fry till golden brown.

Serve hot with a green coriander chutney.

Khade Masale ka Bhuna Gosht

A Delhi Kayasth speciality, this dish also resembles the dry ishtoo of the Shahjahanabad Muslim community. Tomatoes are obviously a later, colonial influence. Typically, this is a slow-cooked dish that would have used just yoghurt for acidity. The coriander seeds add a distinct flavour.

INGREDIENTS

Oil
Whole garam masala
- 2 cinnamon sticks
- 4 bay leaves
- 5 black cardamoms
- 6 green cardamoms
- 12 cloves

2 tsp peppercorns
3–4 whole red chillies, deseeded
2 tbsp whole dry coriander seeds
1kg goat meat
4 large onions, sliced thin
2 tbsp chopped ginger
1 tbsp chopped garlic
3 tomatoes, chopped fine
Salt to taste
1 tbsp yoghurt, beaten (optional)

METHOD

Heat oil and add all the garam masala. Sauté.

Then put the meat and the other ingredients, cover and cook till the meat is well done. The meat cooks in its own juice as well as that of the onions.

Once the meat is fully cooked, bhuno it for about 5–10 minutes more on a low flame, adding 2 tbsp of oil and 2 tbsp of beaten yoghurt. This intensifies the flavour.

Mrs LC (left) steering her new daughter-in-law, my mother, through the mandatory music mehfil after the wedding ceremony.

Epilogue

If Music be the Food of Life...

Khana and gana were just two of the dominant ways in which 'being Kayasth' was passed down to me. I was aware of just one of these legacies as I was growing up, an inexplicably angry and rebellious teenager in Lucknow.

Home-cooked Kayasth food was the norm. I took no special notice of it, of the sookhi urad and kofte, of takey paise and pulao, that appeared with unfailing regularity on the table. We very rarely ate any other kind of food. There were virtually no restaurants we frequented – just Royal Café for birthdays, chaat in Aminabad and seekh kebabs from my father's preferred shops near the K.D. Singh Babu Stadium. But I did experiment a fair bit in the kitchen, spurred on by the family but also by a nameless urge within that kept me awake at nights thinking of inventive ways in which I could turn out cakes and desserts, or even just fashion rotis into crisp chips.

In one memorable instance that left my parents aghast and sent them scurrying to the grocer's the next day, I came up with a fancier way to serve and eat Marie biscuits – with a dollop of red toothpaste on top since the jam that could dress up the treat had run out! On better nights I could turn out quite a decent 'pineapple surprise', a confection of canned pineapple, gelatin and cream all whipped together. A keeper of many diaries, I had one devoted to cake recipes, in which I would meticulously paste all the recipes I had cut out from *Women's Era* or the *Dalda Cookbook* or whichever resource presented itself to me in my small-town world. I found ways to improvise Greek yoghurt cakes, jammy Swiss rolls, pound cakes and English trifles. On my fifteenth birthday, I was gifted a good oven. On my sixteenth, it was an imported hand blender, such fancy gadgetry not yet available in pre-liberalization Lucknow.

Because the table at home unfailingly bore 'regular' Kayasth khana, I suppose these were excursions to escape that context, to invent a new reality for myself. Though, of course, in trying to break tradition, I was only following the tradition of Kayasth life, which looked constantly to reinvent itself! But I didn't think of it that way then.

Music, on the other hand, was the obvious way in which the elders sought to instil Kayasth-ness into me. There was no escape from the legacy. The first bhajan Barima ever taught me was a simple two-line ode to Krishna. I learnt it as a six-year-old. The next year, Masterji was hired to come home every Monday to teach me the basics of

Hindustani classical music. The training would continue for the next ten years in an unvarying ritual that involved a strict guru, a floundering, indisciplined student and an indulgent but firm grandmother whose presence loomed large over the classes even when she was physically away. Every few weeks, I would write detailed letters to Barima, telling her in detail about the new raags I had learned. Every few months when Barima and Papa would visit us, the afternoons would invariably be spent learning a song or two from her diary.

Barima's 'gane ki diary' was her treasure trove. Handwritten in it were the thousand-plus songs that she knew. Not the classical bandishes (those were left to gurujis and masterjis like mine who were called upon to impart formal training), but the special-occasion songs – bhajans, holis, mehendis, even the relatively less popular forms of wedding and folk songs such as the sehras, banna-bannis, teej songs to welcome the rains, kajris and, finally, the qawwalis and ghazals that had made Barima so popular in her club circle. Some songs went back to Barima's childhood and were traditional Mathur songs. Others had been picked up from various people – relatives and friends – on occasions such as Railway Club mehfils, the annual Mathur functions and weddings. Still others had been 'composed' by Barima and Papa, the perfectly matched duo. He, the writer, penned lyrics for every social occasion; she set them to music. The tunes ranged from older bhajans and ghazals to sonorous film songs.

The singer Mukesh's 'Chaand si mehbooba', from the film *Himalaya ki God Mein*, became institutionalized in the LCs' world as 'Chaand si bahurani', a song to welcome a new bride into the family. Similarly, 'Tere pyaar ko is tarah se bhulana', from the film *Maine Jeena Seekh Liya*, also sung by Mukesh, became a powerful song sung by Mrs LC on her own fiftieth wedding anniversary function.

Mukesh was a hot favourite with my grandparents. Some of his 'private' ghazals were zealously guarded by Barima, as though they were her own. Requests for these lyrics by other music lovers and singers were firmly turned down. Barima taught me these songs on the strict condition that I would not pass on to anyone, at the many social functions where we sang them, the little sheets of paper on which the notations and lyrics had been written. Other Kayasth homes may have listened to records of Begum Akhtar and Bade Ghulam Ali Sahib, and may or may not have tried to sing those songs, but the LCs were partial to Mukesh. Not just because he was of their generation and a popular singer, but also because he belonged to the same Kayasth community as them! He was a Mathur and my grandparents were proud of the fact, even if the family connection (it seems there was one) was a very distant one.

One of my favourite memories of coming back from school is finding my grandparents in our little garden, basking in the sun, eating roasted peanuts and guava, their favourite fruit, with black rock salt. We, the children, would happily join the feast, sitting with faces away from the sun (lest we got tanned), as per Barima's injunction. We would chat about this and that, and our grandparents would join in, discussing the names of various flowers in the garden or how to keep the score in tennis, or recounting stories of feasts in the good old days, and so on. I loved those conversations.

Our grandparents always conversed with us as equals. I was never talked down to, even though arguments were not encouraged and any questioning of his views irked LC in particular. At these times, Barima played peacemaker, switching to teaching me songs when conversations became a trifle heated. When we had basked enough in the sun, we would move indoors to my grandparents' room where I would lie between them on the bed, chatting. During these interludes, Barima sometimes hummed different songs from the diary so that I would at least get acquainted with the tunes.

It was Barima's aim, she said, to teach me all the songs from her diary, from the beginning to the end. Given that there were no notations, just the lyrics, this was quite a task. The fact that I wasn't the most dedicated of students, made the task even more challenging. If I played truant with Masterji, never doing my riyaaz, I was hardly much better with Barima. I was reasonably able to stick to the sur, melody, and taal, rhythm. But I just didn't want to learn!

Before any wedding or Diwali function or simply visits from relatives at home, my training sessions with Barima would become more vigorous and formal. She would order me to bring out her harmonium (which had already been passed on to me as her legacy) and the tanpura on which my mother and her younger sister had learned music as teenagers. I would be made to practise 'properly' so that I could deliver a flawless performance at the functions, which were fairly competitive. Each Kayasth singer at these soirées would want to hold centre stage, making sure that his/her song so dominated the evening that all other numbers that followed seemed *pheeka* – pale, flavourless – in contrast. Barima dragged me to all such weddings and cultural festivities. I sang everywhere, ending up ecstatic when I dominated, dismayed when I couldn't do so – and always stressed about performing.

As a three-year-old in Banaras, when my doting but domineering grandmother held a glass of milk to my mouth, it had always been with the exhortation to finish fast because, somewhere, an imaginary child would otherwise beat me to it. The exhortation to learn music followed much the same tack. I needed to compete and show off my 'talent'.

Since I was deemed talented, or at least to possess enough musical potential, legacies were bestowed on me, one by one. My mother's tanpura had already been brought down from Bareilly and handed over to me. It was a prized possession. It had been procured from Miraj – the town famous for making the best stringed musical instruments – by my nana. Even in the musical world of the Mathur Kayasths, where every home had a harmonium and a tabla, this qualitatively superior tanpura from Miraj was a big deal.

In the middle of the nineteenth century, instruments like the sitar and the tanpura were only made in Banaras or Calcutta. A Muslim sword-maker from Bijapur, called Faridsaheb, had been summoned by the Nizam to make the metal *kalash,* the inverted arches or 'pots', common to Islamic architecture in the subcontinent, at the dargah of Khwaja Meersaheb in Miraj. Faridsaheb and his family came to this town and eventually started making both weapons for the princely ruler and repairing musical instruments for musicians patronized by him. Eventually, as the British banned weapon-making, the family shifted their focus to making stringed instruments and founded an entire tradition of craftsmanship in that little town of central India. My mother's tanpura had been bought at a hefty price from the best shop there. I am not sure whether it was the same one that Faridsaheb had founded. But I remember what an honour it was, when, at fourteen years of age, I was given that tanpura and told to take care of it.

Barima had another legacy that she wanted to eventually pass on to me. The music diary. Since hers was fairly tattered by that time, she embarked upon an ambitious project: to write me my own. It was a slow and painful process for her arthritic fingers, but she was determined that she would complete the tome.

'Meri pyaari beti Rini ko Barima ka sanchit khazana,' 'To my darling daughter, Rini, Barima's trove of treasure.'

the inscription began, Barima addressing me by my 'pet' name, Rini – bestowed upon me because the family were big fans of the flawless English diction of Rini Simon, the newsreader on television, at the time I was born!

Was I going to be worthy of its possession?

Before she would pass on her diary, Barima was clear that I had to be equal to the task. When Masterji came for the lessons, she never failed to sit in and listen, instructing him on how to instruct me! All my performances were judged severely. Even on days when I thought I had sung well enough, Barima would shake her head and say that I had sung 'flat' – without the *murkis*, the rounded curves at the end of notes, that define a classically trained voice, separating it from the singing of untrained novices. If you pitched your voice, it was crucial for it to 'stick to the correct note'; there was to be no wavering, no ifs and buts – just the perfection of the voice finding the precise note like a sharply shot arrow. As we went through the bhajans and ghazals, through the *tahray hue* (sombre and romantic) evening raags that I developed a fondness for – Malkaus and Kedar and Yaman – the arrow was finding its mark. But the shooter had other aims.

On the erroneous assumption that all 'journalists' were 'writers', I had made up my mind to pursue print journalism. But writing needed life experiences and life was waiting to be experienced outside Lucknow. Delhi University beckoned. My parents agreed to the plan, but with a proviso: I had to secure a seat in a top college along with hostel accommodation, a tough proposition. Luckily, the brainwashing at Vasudevan Uncle's tutorials for science and maths had enabled me to opt for that killer combo of physics–chemistry–math–biology (PCMB) for my Class 12 exams – even though it was always English literature and the humanities I had aced in school before that. But PCMB meant that I scored enough to make the cut-offs, and the family was happy enough with my choice of Lady Shri Ram College.

For me however, college was like a bucket of ice-cold water being thrown at my face. I had always done well in school, both academically and in other activities, from creative writing to debating. Here I was now, finally studying English literature, my favourite subject. But being surrounded by classmates who had been the cream of the crop in their schools woke me up to how randomly I had read till then, how much there was to know, how little I really knew. There was a whole wide world out there in which this gauche Lucknowi just didn't fit. I took all the creative writing classes possible, attempted automatic poetry writing, tried to copy Rushdie for a while, read up impossibly boring works in the library, studied hard so that I landed up topping the university (a nerdish badge of shame, surely) and in general tried desperately to reinvent myself as a literary sophisticate.

In between, I had my first sizzler, my first Nirula's burger, 'van Chinese' and even a terribly sophisticated grilled chicken breast at the rooftop grill restaurant in what used to be Delhi's Holiday Inn. I had dared not order a complicated grilled lobster there for fear of not being able to manage the shell, but it was a meal to remember, nevertheless. In all of this being Kayasth was gradually forgotten. Kaliya and kebab and certainly music lessons were not a part of the new identity I was fashioning for myself. Meanwhile, the diary had been finished. But Barima, perhaps disappointed by the path I was sauntering along, refrained from giving it to me.

Diaries are powerful things. Even musical ones, sans notations. They reveal to us not just what is written on their surfaces but also what may have been in the mind, grazing just below. The inscription on the diary has several scratches. You can almost follow the tortuous workings of Barima's mind, now unravelling after a stroke, as she scratches out my name, and puts instead my cousin's – a worthier inheritor of the legacy, she may have felt for a time. But then, she seems to change her mind, and the cousin's name is crossed out and mine put back, and then mine scratched and the cousin's inserted. This happens a few more times, till, once again, it is my name on the diary.

As a trainee sub-editor with a national daily and then a cub reporter, I had other ambitions to follow than mastering Kayasth khana and gana. But it seems as if I have come around after traversing along a wide circle. For Barima eventually left her diary to me. As also, perhaps, some of her sense of self.

Acknowledgements

A heapful of gratitude to many Kayasths and a few non.

To Poulomi Chaterjee, editor extraordinaire: ever patient, ever warm, ever sensitive to writerly whimsies. This book could not have been completed without your hand-holding and your eye for detail. I will miss our meandering discussions in Meherchand Colony Market.

To Manu Chandra, who has had a strangely similar upbringing to mine (including the presence of a doting Kayasth granny) and who was the only one I trusted with the first draft. He took it upon himself to line-edit it in between opening restaurants and cooking up storms. All your suggestions have found a place here.

To Amrita Swarup, who shared fantastic, khandani stories of growing up in a palatial home by the Ganga and of never-ending khana-peena. The vino, sheermal and kebab we shared have (hopefully) not been in vain.

To Priyanka Saxena Ray, Rai Mahimapat Ray and Nutan Ray for insights into the landed Kayasthness of eastern Uttar

Pradesh, at once familiar and different from the workings and cooking of my own home.

To Prabhas Kumar for memories of grand bureaucrats and for showing me an invaluable treasure in the first etched copy of the Constitution of India.

To Anil and Kumi Chandra for yakhni pulao and conversations, which triggered new thoughts, and for inadvertent insights into Kayasthness.

To Anjali and Rajesh Dayal for reliving their memories of Daryaganj and Shahar. To Usha Kishore Baghwala for feeding me nargisi kofte and sharing recipes.

To my chachi, Minoo Rishi, whose bhuna meat and pabri kofte have helped us take the khana of our home into the outer world...

Many thanks also to Vatsala Kaul Banerjee for translating the scattered Hindi verses in the book.

To my family Rajeev, Beena, Aaliya and Ashwin, who are within this narrative and within me even if I don't mention them. There would be no food and no memories without you. This book is for you.

And, above all, to Mrs LC herself, for managing to instil in me, the most reluctant Kayasth ever, some of her tradition however much I chose to run away from it. The irony of me writing this book can perhaps only be appreciated by her. Wherever you are, Barima, you must be smiling.